4.95

Guide to
Student Life
AWAY FROM HOME

Guide to
Student Life
AWAY FROM HOME

GRAHAM JONES

David & Charles
Newton Abbot London North Pomfret (Vt)

British Library Cataloguing in Publication Data

Jones, Graham
  Guide to student life away from home.
  1. College students' socio-economic status —
  Great Britain
  I. Title
  378'.198   LB3605

ISBN 0 7153 8211 X (Hardback)

Typeset by Typesetters (Birmingham) Limited
and printed in Great Britain
by Redwood Burn Limited, Trowbridge
for David & Charles (Publishers) Limited
Brunel House   Newton Abbot   Devon

Published in the United States of America
by David & Charles Inc
North Pomfret   Vermont 05053   USA

Contents

TO MY PARENTS

The author
Graham Jones is a journalist who has specialised in reporting on higher education matters and medicine. He graduated in Human Biology from the University of Surrey in 1978, and was editor of the university's Union Handbook in 1976. He now lives in Guildford.

Acknowledgements
The line illustrations are the work of Trevor Ridley.
The maps are based upon plans supplied by the Automobile Association and are reproduced with the permission of the Controller of Her Majesty's Stationery Office. *Crown Copyright Reserved.*
Photographs are by A. F. Kersting.

Introduction

Today's students are generally vocationally minded, sensible adults. Some may have wild parties, a few do take drugs, and sometimes they do discuss philosophy. But most of the time they are hard at work racing against time to learn as much as possible before impending, all important, exams.

Students are expected to work hard, learn fast, and to pass exams. It is therefore vital that you go to university or college with the intention to learn. If you do not then you will soon be discovered by the authorities and your college career may be brought to an end.

Life at a university, polytechnic or college, will be different from anything you have experienced before. You will be completely on your own. Possibly for the first time in your life you will have to make decisions yourself.

This guide will help you. It has been written to point you in the right direction for a successful time at college.

It is not my intention to dictate how you should behave, nor does this book pretend to contain all the answers to the problems you will be faced with. 'Student Life Away from Home' is just a guide to help you through.

It has been assumed that you have already applied for a place at a university, polytechnic, or college.

I hope that this book will prove of value to school leavers and first year students. However, you will almost certainly find this book useful throughout your student days.

The Gardner Arts Centre, Sussex University

In the second week of August each year, the hearts of thousands of school leavers beat faster as they wait for the brown manilla envelope which contains their A Level results. For most, the results will be what they expected. For some there will be disappointment, and for others there may well be a pleasant surprise.

If your results match the offer already made to you by a university or polytechnic then your action is simply to confirm your acceptance. On the other hand, if your results are not good enough to get the place you wanted then the decision making is a little harder.

If you have passed some A Levels but your grades are not high enough for you to take up the place you wanted, you can still manage to go to university. The 'Clearing Scheme' comes into operation every autumn for students who did not make it into university the first time around. This scheme is run by the Universities Central Council on Admissions (UCCA), which will have administered your initial application. Basically the scheme allows students who were unable to get the required grades for their offered places to get a place at another university through clearing.

Most courses at all universities will have spare places to fill. Each university notifies UCCA of the places they have available

1 Preparing to Go

and in return UCCA will send them a list of candidates still seeking a course. The universities can then arrange interviews for suitable students in September.

If you have failed to get a place at your chosen university it is best to register straight away with the UCCA clearing scheme, though UCCA will automatically send you details.

If you have failed to get a place offered to you by a polytechnic, life is a little harder. There is no central admissions unit for polytechnics and so you will have to write around the various colleges asking if they have spare places.

If you have failed to get the required number of A Levels to merit admission to university or a polytechnic then there are a number of alternatives available. One is to go back to school for another year to retake your A Levels. You could also take them again by going to a technical college or evening classes.

Another solution would be to enter a less demanding field of higher education, such as a diploma course. Finally, you could give up the whole idea of furthering your education and go straight into a job. The right decision can only be reached by careful consideration and by talks with your parents, friends, teachers, and also your careers advisers.

Once you have confirmed your acceptance of a university place it will be a couple of weeks before you hear anything further.

Most of this time will probably be spent worrying about what will happen at university, and whether or not you will be able to cope on your own away from your parents.

While waiting to hear from the university or college there is one important thing which must be done, and that is to ensure that your local education authority knows where you are going. If you fail to do this you will not receive your grant cheque. You should have applied for a grant during your last year at school. If you have not applied then do so immediately, as the administration involved takes some time. You should also apply to other sources of finance such as professional institutes and large companies.

In due course, about two or three weeks before the start of term, you will receive a parcel from the university. This will probably contain a letter welcoming you to the university and confirming your place, plus a number of booklets, leaflets and letters, all of which should be read carefully. You will also receive a university prospectus, a student handbook, and information about accommodation, careers, insurance and banking.

Sometimes the parcel will also contain a guide to what may be called 'Introduction Week', or 'Induction'. This is sometimes known as 'Freshers Week' and is now operated by most universities as a means of allowing new students to get to know the university and settle in before the term begins. 'Intro Week' takes place in the few days immediately before the start of the autumn term.

Before you can attend 'Intro Week', though, you must have somewhere to live. One of the most important booklets which will have been sent will be that concerning accommodation.

Campus universities usually provide on-site accommodation for all first year students. Many of the non-campus colleges and universities also provide purpose built accommodation in the town for first year students. Collegiate universities such as Oxford or Durham often provide rooms in the college for new students. Regardless of the type of university you will be attending, it is important to apply for the type of accommodation that you think will suit you best.

Campus universities provide a range of residences from self-catering to full board accommodation. There is a growing trend towards self-catering accommodation as it has proved cheaper to run and also gives the students more freedom and independence. This style of residence usually consists of a group of study bedrooms with a central communal area. This central area provides all the facilities for cooking and is also the social centre of the building. But for those students who do not wish to cook for themselves, or who cannot cook, universities with self-catering accommodation also offer central catering facilities run on cafeteria lines. However, many students find it more convenient, and often more economical, to cook for themselves and, indeed, self-catering can be a lot of fun too.

Some halls of residence have dining halls where meals are provided by the university, and there are no self-catering facilities, or at best they are very limited. Such halls have more expensive rents as the charges for the meals are often included. For those students who do not wish to cater for themselves such halls are ideal. There is however a move away from this traditional style of hall as it is now considered to be too much like boarding school and curbs the independence of the individual student.

Do not, of course, opt for the full board style of accommodation if you hate the rigid timetable of school. Similarly, if you detest cooking then do not choose self-catering residences. Decide on the type of residence to suit you best and do not choose something because the photograph in the prospectus looks good — this could be misleading! Once you have made up your mind let the university know immediately. They will have sent you an application form for this purpose. Be prepared, though, to accept a form of residence which you did not ask for. Every year certain styles of residence are over-applied for and consequently some people have to be disappointed.

Also, universities cannot always provide accommodation for all students in purpose built university-owned buildings. In this case you will have to find somewhere to live in the town. Finding somewhere to live in a strange town is a difficult task and for this reason much of the universities' own accommodation is reserved for first year students, leaving the second and third years, who have spent some time in the area, to make their own arrangements.

If a situation arises where you do have to find somewhere to live on your own, do seek advice first. Ask the accommodation officer at the university what is available and where to look. Also ask the officer what to avoid, something which the student union can help with too.

Having found out what is available and decided what type of accommodation is most suitable, visit the town and look at possible places to stay. It is unwise to try and find somewhere to live by postal applications. Every year thousands of students find themselves homeless at the beginning of the academic year. In many instances this is because there is a lack of suitable accommodation, but some cases are due to the fact that the students wasted time before they started looking seriously. Accommodation is short in university towns, so start searching as soon as possible.

Most first year students will not have to face the task of looking for lodgings. It is unwise for new students to look for lodgings by choice, rather than to apply for university accommodation, as it is much easier to tackle university life without the additional worry of having to find somewhere to live. If, at the start of term, you do find that you are homeless, seek immediate advice from the accommodation officer and the student union. Together they will be able to find you some temporary accommodation. Once you have applied for your accommodation there are a number of other important matters with which you must deal.

While at university you will have to manage your own finances. You will be expected to pay the rent on time, buy food, books and stationery, and you will need cash to see you through day-to-day expenses.

Your grant will be sent to the university to arrive at or near the beginning of term. It will be in the form of a cheque made payable to you and consequently it is essential to have a bank cheque account which is operational before you start university. It is up to you to choose whether to open an account at a bank branch near your home or near your university. Banks near colleges often provide a range of services and have a student accounts officer, or an account can be opened through the post.

Your parcel of information from the university will contain a list of all the local banks, some of which may be in the university buildings or on the campus. You should apply to open a cheque account (or current account) in the first instance. This is the type of account which you can pay money into at any time, at any branch of any bank. You will be issued with a cheque book which can be used to pay for goods or to draw cash. If you present a cheque for cash at the branch shown on the cheque the cashier will give you the money, which will then be deducted from your account. To withdraw cash from other branches, or from other banks, you will need a cheque guarantee facility. Cheque guarantee cards are not issued automatically so you will need to see the bank manager about getting one. The cards guarantee that your cheques up to £50 will be honoured by the bank. Chapter 4 goes into detail about your banking needs.

One of the first items to be paid out of your grant will be the rent. The rest of the money will have to cover food, books, clothes, stationery and social spending. Many students forget to budget for one important item — insurance.

While living at home your personal belongings are protected against damage and theft under your parents' insurance policies. Now that you are setting up on your own this protection expires and alternative arrangements must be made. Student residences are not immune from danger. The rooms can be broken into and fires can occur. Make sure that you do not overlook the need for insurance when you have arrived at the university (see chapter 4).

Once you have found somewhere to live, opened a bank account, made sure that you will be financed by a grant or by your parents, and considered the need for insurance, you will be in a position to organise some less important, but nevertheless necessary, matters. You will want to find out what to take with you, when to arrive, and where to go when you get there.

Every year many first year students arrive in the wrong place at the wrong time, and often with the wrong things! This is usually simply because they did not bother to find out what they really needed to know.

The university will send you everything you need to know, including a map of the town, a programme of events on the first day, and so on. Read all this information with great care and remember it. Not only has it been written to help you, it is also intended to help the university reduce the amount of time spent in dealing with late arrivals and lost people!

Check up on what to take with you. Many students arrive with too much luggage. There is no need, for example, to take sheets and blankets *if* they are going to be provided by the university. You will probably be sent a check-list of essential items. The local education authorities usually allow first year students a small advance on their grants to buy anything necessary. A typical check-list might include such items as: cooking utensils, cutlery, sheets, towels and tea towels. In addition, take enough food to last you a day or two, soap, toothpaste, and a toilet roll! If you are going to stay in hall you really will need very little other than your personal belongings.

Also, check what items you will need for your course. Medical students might need a microscope, and linguistic students might need a cassette tape recorder. Some universities have arranged special discount schemes through which you can buy such equipment. It is worth finding out if such a scheme operates for your course, and you could also consider buying second-hand equipment from older students.

Having decided what to take it is sometimes easier if you send the bulk of your luggage in advance. You can send a trunk to the university via British Rail or one of the road haulage services and then collect it when you arrive. This will avoid the necessity of carrying a large amount of luggage.

Once you have organised the practical side of getting yourself ready to go to university it is important to prepare yourself psychologically. You need to be aware of what will happen when you arrive and what problems are likely to be encountered.

Naturally, by reading all the information the university has sent to you the job of psychological preparation will be well under way; but if you do not know what will happen on the first day you will feel lost, homesick, and generally depressed. That, certainly, is not the way to start out on a challenging career at university.

2 Coping to Begin With

The Science Block, York University

At the end of September, or thereabouts, the big day will arrive. You will probably have spent most of the previous night awake, either through worry, or perhaps due to one too many farewell drinks!

Plan to arrive at the university by mid-afternoon. This is generally the most convenient time for you and the university. In addition, there is usually a large number of people milling around and so you are less likely to feel lonely. The university will have told you in advance about the arrangements for your first day. Follow this carefully prepared plan as it will ensure that the day runs smoothly.

If you arrive during the afternoon and the place looks deserted you have probably arrived on the wrong day. Every year, new students turn up at their hall of residence a day or so earlier than they should. This happens with startling regularity and is usually because these new students simply have not checked their dates.

If you do go on the wrong day you must be prepared to suffer

any consequences, such as being asked to come back on the correct day. Generally speaking, though, you will be able to stay even though it may take some time to sort out accommodation. Often, student residences are used by conference visitors during vacation time, so if you arrive early it is possible that your allocated room will be occupied. And when you are found somewhere temporary to stay you will have to put up with being totally alone until the rest of your year arrives.

On the first day of Intro Week universities are crowded. Parents, brothers and sisters, girlfriends and boyfriends all seem to want to get in on the act of helping new students settle in. The stairs of halls of residences are crammed with the two-way traffic of families unloading cars and carrying suitcases. Inevitably, there is total confusion! For a start everyone is completely lost. Some new students even find themselves turning up in the wrong rooms and having to make embarrassed apologies.

In addition, there are the students who arrive at the wrong hall of residence. This always throws just about everything into

chaos. The warden of the hall searches desperately for the right
name on his list and then has the awesome task of trying to find
out where this misplaced student really should be. Meanwhile a
queue of new students wait for their room keys and car parking
problems build up. But, despite difficulties and embarrassments,
everyone is usually in the right place by the early evening —
quite often by sheer luck.

When you arrive and have been issued with your keys you will
become part of this general confusion. The best thing to do is to
get on with the job of unloading the car as quickly as possible. It
is always a good idea to move the car away after unloading and to
park nearby, rather than leave it in the immediate area of the
residence. It is only fair that later arrivals with bags to carry
should be allowed to park as near as possible to the residence. Of
course, new students who arrive by bus or train can just claim
their keys and go straight to their rooms with the minimum of
fuss and bother.

Once you have taken every bag, suitcase and box to your room
you can get on with the unpacking. But if your family is there
you may not wish to do this. Most people find it easier to unpack
their bags alone. It is quite simply much easier and probably
much faster. If this is what you want to do then make it clear to
your parents, but do not make it sound as though you are trying
to get rid of them as soon as possible!

For many new students, and for quite a few parents too, the
imminent farewells are somewhat daunting. Generally, leaving
home to join university is the first time that any teenager will
have been away from his or her parents for longer than a holiday.
Now the new students and the parents have to face a three month
separation. The prospect can be depressing and it is not unusual
to see mothers departing from the university grounds with tears
in their eyes on the first day of Introduction Week. Many new
students will also feel depressed at the thought of being separated
from what has certainly been a rather cosy arrangement for the
last eighteen years.

Nevertheless, it has to be done. The best way is probably to say
a fond au-revoir in your room and then to let your family make
their own way out of the building instead of, say, going down to
the car and waving them off. This sounds a little cold but going
to university is a major break from what you and your family
have been used to, and going back to the car will put you all in

the wrong psychological framework for your first parting. You will all, subconsciously, be expecting to drive off together. And, because you do not, it will only increase distress on both sides.

So now you are alone in your room with a collection of bags and boxes. What next? If, like most students, you have a radio, then unpack that first. Some music and a friendly voice in the background is a boon to unpacking. And it also stops you feeling lonely.

At about twenty universities there are University Radio Stations. these are small, closed circuit radio stations run by volunteers and they broadcast in the medium waveband. Most of them are on 312 metres (963 kiloHertz). If your university has such a radio station then it is an excellent idea to tune into that straight away. The stations generally broadcast throughout Introduction Week and are often very helpful for new students. They publicise the events of the week and are very good at keeping you in touch with what is going on.

You might also find that the BBC, or a commercial company, has a local radio station in the area. Some of these stations operate a student information service, so while you are unpacking is as good a time as any to listen in.

Unpacking can take quite a long time. You will change your mind repeatedly as to where to put things and get thoroughly fed up with the apparent lack of space. Eventually, when everything is in its place, you will start wondering what to do next.

The best thing to do at this rather difficult point is to find someone to talk to. Introduce yourself to the student in the next room, or go to the communal room, or kitchen, and talk to whoever is there. If you have timed your arrival at university correctly then you will probably finish unpacking round about tea-time. So it is a good opportunity to get to know a couple of fellow first years by going to the restaurant for something to eat. Then, if you are shy and cannot think of anything to say you can eat your meal slowly and only speak when your mouth is not full! Making new friends cannot be done instantly but acquaintance with one or two students on your first day will help you to settle in faster.

Most universities have some form of social gathering for first year students on the first night of Introduction Week. These events vary from formal dinners to discos, cheese and wine evenings or coffee evenings. Whichever form of reception takes place at your university, do not miss it. These social events are often arranged by each hall of residence and they are usually supplemented by some gathering for the whole university which is organised by the student union.

At all of these receptions there will be second year and final year students as well as university staff and officials. These people will circulate in the crowd and make sure that the first years start chatting. If you want to have a successful Introduction Week then do not stand silent at the reception. The more friends you make the happier you will be.

Your first night at university will be unique, so do not judge university life on the basis of this single experience. However, it is not unknown for a number of new students to 'drop out' before Introduction Week has ended. And a few more give up the whole idea of university after a few days of their degree course proper.

It is quite impossible to decide whether or not you can cope without your parents after such a short time away from home. If, after some time at university, you cannot face it any more then talk to your lecturers, friends and parents to help you decide whether or not to stay on.

You will not want to consider such action on your first night. In the early part of your university career you will naturally feel homesick, and at no time more homesick than on the first night of Introduction Week. Homesickness is not easily overcome and there is no simple solution. The best method is to occupy yourself so fully that you do not have time to think about being away from home. So on your first night it is very important to take part in all the activities which have been organised.

The social events will probably end well before the union bar or pub closes. As in most universities the union bar is the social centre it would be worthwhile making a visit. This will achieve two things. First, you will not be lonely in your room; second, it will give you a chance to meet some more people and perhaps make some new friends. There is no need to be shy . . . they are all in the same boat!

Despite the obvious attraction of drinking with new found friends in a bar which is likely to have been granted an extension of normal licensing hours, it is not wise to drink too much. The next day you will need to be up and about quite early for your introduction to your academic department, the lecturers and your course.

Before going to bed on the first night, make sure that you are prepared for the morning. You will want a notebook and a pen at the very least, but be certain to have anything else which might be needed for your specific course. If you set out everything in advance, there will be no need to rush around in the morning.

What happens when you first visit your department will vary according to the type of university at which you are studying and also the course for which you are registered. For example, if you are one of three people studying Chinese philosophy at a small college you are likely to receive a very different reception from one of a hundred students studying civil engineering at a large technological university.

Generally, though, you will be introduced to your lecturers and given a brief description of your course. Do not attempt to take everything in at this stage. These initial meetings are really

only to help you settle in and the basic facts will almost certainly
be repeated during the first couple of weeks.

The first day in the department will, however, be useful. You
will be able to introduce yourself to your fellow students and
have an opportunity to meet your personal tutor. He or she will
be one of your lecturers who will watch over and help you
through your years at university. Personal tutors vary in their
attitudes but they generally give advice about your course and
will help you cope with any academic problems. In addition,
they will also help and advise should any personal problems
arise.

On your first day it is not likely that you will be asked to do any
academic work. However, some courses have introduced
'academic exercises' in which students are set some problem
which they have to solve, usually in small groups. This gets new
students thinking in their own discipline and often marks the
formation of new friendships.

In addition to the general introduction and any minor
academic exercises, you will also be given a reading list and
general advice about items needed for your course. Although you
may be tempted, do not under any circumstances rush out to the
bookshop and buy all the books on your reading list. The
university will have a well stocked library and, besides, your
grant would not last more than a week or two if you spent all of it
on books.

On the other hand, if you do not buy any books then you are
not likely to learn very much. You will need certain texts and
some basic reference books, but your reading list should state
which ones are vital. If your list does not help, then find out from
your personal tutor, lecturers, and students in years above you.

Your department will also advise you about any equipment
that may be necessary for your course. For example, biology
students will need a dissection kit, students of electronics will
need a soldering iron, and linguistics students might need a
portable cassette tape recorder. In any event, try to find out the
best method of buying equipment — the department or the
student union might have some form of discount scheme, or a
second-hand shop. If your lecturers do not tell you where you
can buy the items for your course, then ask them.

One item which will certainly be distributed free of charge to all
students is the course timetable. Unlike rigid school timetables,

those at universities are not crammed with compulsory lessons; they consist of a combination of lectures, tutorials, seminars and practical classes. Your timetable may well vary from week to week and you will be left on your own much of the time with very little programmed for you to attend.

Lectures are the nearest you will get to school lessons. They are the rather formal meetings where a lecturer imparts information about a particular subject. But, unlike school, university lectures are not intended to cover everything which you should learn. Rather, they point you in the right direction to study on your own.

Tutorials are meetings of a small group of students with one or two lecturers. These meetings usually take the form of discussion about certain topics and are also used to monitor your progress through your course.

Seminars are meetings of a larger number of students than seen in a tutorial, although not necessarily attended by the number of students seen in lectures. At a seminar you will be expected to talk for a specific period of time about one particular aspect of your studies and to answer questions about it.

Other timetable events include practical classes and laboratory meetings. Generally speaking, it is only these parts of your course, and tutorials, which are compulsory. In most cases you will find that all the other aspects of organised study are subject to your own initiative and inclination. This does not mean, though, that you should become lazy and avoid lectures! You should appreciate that the responsibility for organising your studies has been shifted from lecturers to individual students. The amount of work done is now up to you. You will soon learn to adapt to this new way of studying but, until you are able to decide what to study, you will be better off by going to all the lectures and strictly following the timetable.

Having been told about your course in detail you will probably be left free for the remainder of Introduction Week. This is so that you can settle in to your new environment and familiarise yourself with the university, the student union and the town.

An enormous range of activities will have been organised to help you to get to know as much as possible. But, because of the limited time, you will no doubt be confused and a little doubtful as to what to do first and which events to attend. The best way to avoid this inevitable confusion is to work out a personal timetable. Whatever happens, make sure you attend as much as possible; after all, there will not be another chance!

The types of event that take place in most typical Introduction Weeks can be roughly divided into a number of categories. Most of the action will be social, although there will also be sporting, political, religious, cultural and artistic events of all kinds. Most of these are organised by the student union and many of the clubs and societies which are responsible for the individual activities will be campaigning for new members.

You will almost certainly want to join the clubs which provide facilities for you to carry on your particular hobbies and pastimes; and if you have any sporting talents you will want to become a member of the relevant society. But do not ignore the possibility of taking up new interests. University clubs cover a very wide range of activities, many of which you probably were not even aware of.

On joining a university club or society you may be asked to pay a small fee for membership. These fees are used to help with running costs, although in many cases the student union pays for much of each club's activities. Because you may well be asked for a membership fee make sure that you do not sign up to join every club . . . you would never afford it!

You should also organise your social life throughout Introduction Week. The early part of each academic year is laden with a large number of social events from discos to formal dinners, from coffee mornings to cheese and wine evenings, and from quiet gatherings in each hall to noisy competitions in the student union.

Along with people in your hall of residence and those on your course, make an attempt to go to as many different events as possible. This will give you the opportunity to meet more people and make new friends as well as making you busy enough to avoid some homesickness. You will be living with your fellow students for the next three or four years, so the better you get to know each other at the beginning of your university career then the happier you will be throughout your course.

For many first year students, especially the men, Introduction Week can become a time of excessive social permissiveness. This is understandable, because first year students have a new found freedom with none of the parental controls and restrictions to which they have been used. Consequently, some students go that

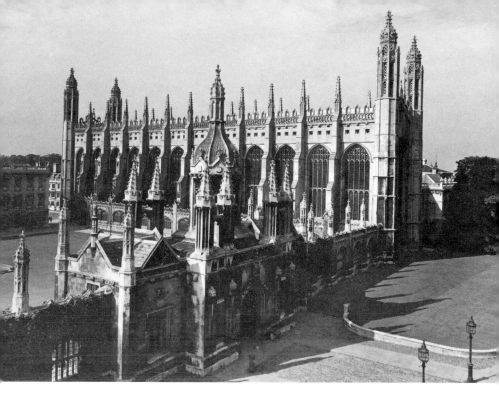

(*above*) King's College Chapel, Cambridge, viewed from the south east. Building of the chapel was started in the fifteenth century; (*below*) The High, Oxford, with Queen's College on the left

(*previous page*) The Great Quadrangle of All Souls College, Oxford. Beyond is the dome of the Radcliffe Camera; (*above*) 'Ye Olde Trip to Jerusalem' Inn at Nottingham is claimed to be the oldest inn in England; (*below*) St George's Hall, Liverpool, is an imposing building in the Greco-Roman style

little bit too far. If you over-indulge during Introduction Week, then learn quickly from your mistakes. Introduction Week will foster self control in your activities and you will soon learn how to look after yourself. It is wise to remember to have a go at everything, but do it in moderation, and enjoy it!

Apart from the jollity, Introduction Week also provides you with enough time to get to know the university and the town. You will soon be able to find your way around the buildings without too much trouble and be able to estimate how long it will take you to get from one part of the university to another. This will help when lectures begin . . . you won't want to miss them!

Go for a walk around the town at some stage during the week. Many students, especially those at campus universities, tend to ignore the town and restrict their activities to the university. However, most university towns offer a wide range of events for students, and even more clubs and societies to join.

Your student union will probably issue you with some information about your particular town and you will also find maps of twenty other university towns in this book. These will help you find your way around. You might also find it useful to buy the town guide published by the local authority.

In your first few days at university you should be able to find out where most of the important buildings are situated. Supermarkets, record shops, boutiques, cinemas, theatres, libraries, public houses, and of course public lavatories, are all used by students and you will need to know where the best ones are. The sooner you get to know the town then the sooner you will feel at home.

It is also a good idea to buy regularly a copy of the local newspaper. A good local newspaper always reflects the town and its atmosphere, and a surprising amount of information can be extracted by a quick read.

By the time the end of Introduction Week comes around you will be amazed at the number of activities you have crammed into such a short time. You will have arrived, unpacked, settled into your room, met new friends, learnt the details of your course, joined a host of clubs and societies, explored the university and the town, and probably recovered from a string of late nights, leaving you almost ready for your first real taste of university when lectures begin.

3 Studying

The Gate of Honour, Caius College, Cambridge

At 9am on the Monday after Introduction Week you will probably be sitting, bleary eyed, in a lecture theatre, ready for the proper beginning of your academic life. You will begin to think to yourself, as you yawn for the umpteenth time, 'Is this really what I came to university for?'

Well, the truthful answer is 'yes'. You have decided to attend university to learn more about your chosen subject. You have started a three year project of reading, writing, talking and listening, focused on one particular range of facts and figures. The main purpose, which you must never lose sight of, is to pass your final examinations and graduate, and to that end you must study successfully.

Many researchers, both here and in the United States, have shown that those students who follow a regular plan, or time-table, are those who tend to achieve the best academic results. Unlike school, as we saw in the last chapter, the responsibility for organising study time is now firmly in your own hands. If you do not have a personal timetable you will probably spend much of your time watching television, propping up the bar, or just idly chatting to students in your hall. You should draw up your own timetable before the first week of term.

If you wait a few days before beginning to operate your individual timetable then you will fall into the trap of believing that there is no need for one and consequently end up time-wasting. You will gradually slide down the slippery slope which leads to fewer attendances at formal timetable events and a poorer performance in examinations.

So, by the end of Introduction Week you should have drawn up a timetable covering organised lectures, tutorials, and so on, as well as any other commitments you may have, such as sporting events and meetings of clubs and societies. You should also include periods for reading, writing and studying on your own. But your timetable must be flexible so that if necessary it can be changed at a moment's notice without upsetting the week's study quota. Since you have probably never had to organise your own studies before it is probably a good idea to follow through the simple example given below which outlines the basic principles involved.

Susan is studying English at a new university in the north of England. During Introduction Week her department issued her with the formal timetable shown on page 32.

DAY / TIME	9am	10	11	12 noon	1 pm	2	3	4
MON	Grammar		Modern literature		L	Language tutorial		
TUE		Shakespeare plays	Literature tutorial		U		Philosophy of language	
WED	Old English	17th century Literature			N			
THUR		Grammar		Literature seminar	C			
FRI		Language seminar			H		Creative writing	

Formal timetable

This is a typical timetable for language students, showing that Susan has twelve hours of organised study each week. She is not compelled to attend everything, but Susan has noted that those students who avoid going to lectures tend to do badly in examinations.

Susan decided that, to begin with at least, she would attend every formal lecture and tutorial. But attendance at formally timetabled events is not enough to pass examinations. In addition, each student is expected to put in many hours of private studying.

So Susan decided to add her own periods of study to her formal timetable and allow for her periods of social activity and sports as shown on page 33.

In this example Susan has carefully slotted in her own study periods around her formal timetable. She has also allowed a number of hours of free time so that the timetable remains flexible, enabling her to complete all her studies each week without having to stick to a rigid work plan.

You will notice that Susan goes through the notes she made in lectures each day and adds notes from her reading. She also ensures that she is prepared for seminars and tutorials by reading about the topics earlier in the day, or on the night before. In the

DAY / TIME	9am	10	11	12 noon	1 pm	2	3	4	5	Evening
MON				Prepare language tutorial	L			Grammar notes	T	Literature notes
TUE	Prepare literature tutorial				U	Shakespeare reading			E	Philosophy notes / Bridge club
WED			Old English notes	Literature notes	N	Hockey Match			A	Prepare literature seminar / Film club
THU	Prepare literature seminar		Grammar notes		C	General reading		Prepare language seminar	→	Hockey training
FRI	Prepare language seminar				H	→		Notes on Creative writing		Disco
SAT					→	Hockey Training/Match			→	
SUN					→	Review of weeks work			→	

Student's personal timetable

evenings she reads about anything she has not understood in lectures. On Sundays she goes over all of the previous week's work and reads about those topics she is interested in which have not been covered in lectures. All this adds about another twenty-five hours of work each week, bringing the total to only thirty-seven hours, less than a working week.

Compare Susan's own timetable with her programme of formal classes to see where she has slotted in her own periods of work. The first important point to notice is that she goes through her lecture notes each day. Always read about the subject of each lecture as soon as possible afterwards. Usually this is only possible in the evening, but do not leave it until the next day. When the topics are fresh in your mind it is easier to learn them.

Susan also goes through each week's work on a Sunday afternoon. This is an excellent example of what you should strive to do. Repetition reinforces everything you have learnt and imprints it in your memory, so when you come to revise for your exams there will be very little hard learning left to do. Revision is not very productive if it is hurried just before examinations. Review your studies each day, at the end of each week, and also on a monthly basis. Susan's flexible timetable allows this continual process of revision to carry on throughout her course and means that her examination performance is likely to be high.

One other principle of organising to note is that Susan has not allocated herself any academic work during lunch hours or tea breaks. She has also left Saturdays and Sunday mornings totally free. This break from work is essential to every student. Each year keen students attempt to spend every waking hour studying. They spend all their available time cramming knowledge into their brains in the hope that the more they have studied the more likely they are to succeed in examinations. This is a false notion and you should not fall into the trap of over-studying.

There is no simple linear relationship between the number of hours spent studying and success in examinations. What is evident, though, is that those students who do not spend any of their time in relaxing, or freeing their mind from the rigours of studying, can do badly in examinations. You must spend a good part of your time in relaxation, socialising and so on. Perhaps the brain becomes clogged and confused if it is over-stimulated with a constant stream of facts and information. Be sure to leave at least one day and a half each week totally free of studies.

So, when organising your individual timetable there are a number of important points to remember. These are:

1 Make sure your timetable fits into the formal plan of classes issued by your department.
2 Allow time for writing up material which has to be handed in, such as essays, practical reports and so on.
3 Read your lecture notes and go through the relevant chapters of books each day after your lectures.
4 Allow time for regular weekly and monthly reviews of your studies.
5 Make your timetable flexible so you can change your plans at a moment's notice.
6 Make sure that you have plenty of free time.

At the end of Introduction Week remember these six points of successful timetabling and organise your own studies around your formal classes and lectures. Having done this you will be well prepared to start an academic career.

Your first lecture will almost certainly be totally confusing. It may well be on a subject which you did not study at school, or it could be just too complicated for you to understand. So it is essential that you take clear, comprehensive notes during such lectures. You can then use these notes in conjunction with text books to learn about the topics mentioned.

A problem for most students is knowing what notes to take and how best to write them. Many people attempt to take down verbatim everything the lecturer says. You will even be able to see some students write down 'Hello, today we are going to look at . . .'. It is a mistake to try and write down everything. Even if you are an extremely fast writer, or can write in some form of shorthand, you are bound to miss an important point.

In every lecture the first priority is listening. The lecturer may well be offering a personal view about a particular topic, or presenting a reasoned argument through various aspects of research or, as is usual, the lecture may be merely a guide to the subjects which you ought to learn properly before your exams. In any case, if you do not listen carefully to what is being said then you will miss important points and consequently the lecture will be of little value. Do not forget that lecturers can sometimes be wrong.

Taking notes in lectures should be just that — jotting down reminders of what the lecturer said. Your notes can then be expanded from text books when you go through them each evening after classes.

Much has been written about the best methods of studying and the most appropriate way of taking notes. People have invented systems of fast note taking and memory-jogging techniques, all of which are bound to have various advantages and disadvantages — some methods will suit some students and not others. Generally, though, a common factor is that the notes should be brief jottings to remind you of what was said in the lecture. Some people refer to such notes as 'keynotes'.

Keynotes are words or short phrases which trigger your memory about what was said at the time you wrote them down. If you expand on your notes each day then there really is no need to write down more than a list of keynotes and phrases in each lecture. This will leave you free to concentrate on what is being said.

Always use loose leaf files for note taking, then you can change the order of your notes at a later date. It also means that material can be added in the correct places. You will then be able to build up a good set of notes for revision, all in one file. If you use a book for taking notes you will not be able to add to them and will have to undertake the rather complicated task of revising from a number of different sets of notes. It is a good idea to use a fresh sheet of loose leaf paper for each lecture. This makes it easier to put your notes in order.

At the top of your fresh sheet of paper write down the main subject of the course of lectures. Underneath this write down the topic to be covered in the individual lecture. You are then ready to listen and write down the first of your keynotes. Follow the lecturer's introductory comments and when he introduces a new topic write down a word or two as a reminder. A few scribbles of explanation can quickly be added if it is a new subject which you do not understand. Within each topic there will be a number of other points which will need noting. Jot keynotes below your main title and in this way you will build up a series of major notes and a whole host of more minor jottings with phrases of explanation.

If a lecture includes visual aid displays of tables, diagrams, or lists, it is not usually necessary to copy these down. Unless specifically told to do so, you probably will not have the time. Most important diagrams and tables will be available in text books and quite often the lecturer will distribute photocopies of the material for you. If you cannot find the relevant item and you are not given a copy then visit your lecturer's office and ask for one. If enough people do the same the lecturer will soon learn about the mistake!

Another point to remember when taking notes is *not* to worry about neatness. You are the only person who is ever going to read them, so it is only necessary to write notes which can be read back easily. Lecture notes will be your main source of revision material and it is more important that they contain the right information than be works of art.

You will see plenty of students with a variety of different coloured pens and pencils making their notes as neat as possible with different coloured underlinings and titles. All the time they spend in prettying up their notes they are missing what the lecturer is saying. Other students spend hours each evening making a fair copy of their rough notes. This only adds time to their studies and usually means that they have to miss out on social activities. There is absolutely no need for this — all you need are legible notes which you can understand and use for revision.

Use the space on your note page to its best advantage and do not cram too many keynotes into each line. Spread your notes around the page, because you will want plenty of space for later additions, after reading text books, and for adding explanations at the end of each day.

Taking notes from books is a lot easier than taking notes in lectures. There is time to re-read paragraphs and go over something which you do not understand. Generally, it is best to read a chapter or section through without making any notes at all, then you can go back over the chapter in detail. It might be an idea to underline relevant paragraphs in pencil as you read.

Your notes from text books should be more than just words and phrases. They should be full explanations of various topics and should be added in the relevant spaces which are available in your lecture notes.

In this way you will gradually build up a comprehensive set of notes about each topic you have to study. You will have notes from lectures, text books and other sources such as research papers. With careful preparation you will need only these for revision.

Far too many students go through their course from day to day with little regard for timetabling and consequently they miss out note taking from text books and general reading. This means that at examination time they have to cram all their essential reading into the time when they really should only be reviewing their work. It is a wise student who works steadily towards examinations, rather than resorting to last minute cramming.

When it comes to revision time your notes should be a major aid. It is therefore essential that you build them up to cover everything which you need to learn. They should be legible to you, accurate and up to date.

The important points to remember are:

1 Use loose leaf paper and files, never exercise books.
2 Use a clean sheet of paper for each lecture.
3 Listen carefully and make a conscious effort to understand.
4 Jot down words and phrases to remind you of important points.

5 Leave plenty of space around your lecture notes.
6 Add to your lecture notes from books on the same day as the lecture.
7 Never re-write lecture notes unless they are almost illegible.
8 Only copy tables and diagrams if told to do so.
9 Update your notes at regular weekly and monthly intervals.

Accurate study notes, however, depend on you reading text books and research papers, and so on, about the particular subjects. You will not have enough money to buy all the books you need, so much of your time will be spent adding to lecture notes from library books. It is therefore essential that you know how to use the library.

You will almost certainly be shown around the library during Introduction Week, but this will be a very brief and, no doubt, a very confusing visit. So during your first few days of studying spend some time on your own familiarising yourself with the library.

Note the layout of the building and find out where the subject books and periodicals for your course are located. Learn how to work the microfilm units and check out the cataloguing system. Look for the photocopying facilities and search out the reference section. Make sure that you know where everything you are likely to need can be found. Often you will find that some university departments have small specialist libraries. Be certain to find your way around these as well.

When you know where your books are located you will be in a much better position to drop into the library for a couple of minutes to check something. A student who does not know his way around the library will have to spend too much time finding books and will not have time to read them.

Another important point about books is knowing how to use them. Unlike school, many of the books used will not be straight text books. Most of them will contain only certain aspects of part of your studies. You will need to be able to locate the right books for your particular subject. To do this compare the tables of contents in a few of the most up to date books on that subject, and then read a small section on a particular topic you understand. If the book explains this well, you will probably find that it treats other topics, including those which you do not understand, in a similar manner.

Other points to remember when choosing a book include noting whether there is an index, who the author is and when the book was written. A recent, well indexed text book by an expert in the subject is more likely to be of help than an out of date book that does not have an index and is written by someone who is not well known in the particular field.

Having chosen the right book many students waste their time by attempting to read it from cover to cover. In some instances this will be necessary, but certainly in the case of text books you need only read particular sections. Text books are not really for sustained reading, they are for using as aids to an understanding of particular topics on an individual basis.

As your time for studying is limited, read only what is essential. You should read about those subjects which have been covered in lectures, those you have been told to study by your lecturers and any others which you do not understand. Much of the time you will not be reading to add to your notes but gathering information to write an essay which in most subjects, is the main form of work which has to be completed for lecturers. Unlike school, you will not simply have to answer a list of questions or complete set pieces of 'homework'. At university you will be expected to write comprehensively on some particular aspect of your course.

The important point to remember when writing essays is to answer the question which has been set. It is not unusual to find students writing about topics very different from those required. If you do not understand what the essay title means then ask the lecturer who set it.

When your mind is clear as to what is required then you can set about researching. Use books, magazines, journals, and so on, to find out as much as possible about the topic. Make notes as you go along, as you would normally when adding to lecture notes from text books.

When you have collected enough facts and background knowledge to write the essay, begin rejecting any material which is not directly relevant to the title of the essay. Having sorted out your information you will need to decide in which order it should be put together. Draw up a plan which outlines what will be included in each paragraph, then work out an introduction and a conclusion, which when read consecutively will summarise the entire essay.

Once you have done this you will be ready to write the first draft copy. When the essay has been completed, leave it for a while and then read it later. This will give your mind a rest from the detailed subject matter and you will be able to spot any mistakes. Make any corrections and then write out a fresh copy to hand in.

Writing up experimental work and research papers is very similar to writing essays. Always follow the same basic principles when completing any written work. These are:

1 Understand exactly what you are required to write about.
2 Research the topic thoroughly.
3 Make careful notes and reject unwanted material.
4 Prepare a detailed plan.
5 Write an introduction and a conclusion which together summarise the entire piece of writing.
6 Always write a draft original and correct it.

Sometimes in a seminar you will be required to read out loud something which you have written. The fault of many students, and a number of lecturers, is that they simply read out their paper in a monotonous voice, with no appreciation of the audience.

When you have to write something for reading at a seminar you need to prepare two versions. The first should be a detailed essay, or report, which is the basis of a more informal summary. The second written work should be bright and lively, and contain all the salient points on the topic.

Never read your summary out word for word. If necessary learn it off by heart. Essays and reports are not written in conversational English, so they tend to sound boring unless presented with some imagination.

The main purpose of studying is to pass examinations, and to get good grades you will need to know what the topics are going to be. You do not need to know exactly what will be asked, but you do need to know which topics will be examined, the style of the questions and how best to answer them. You should find out whether the various examinations are of an essay type, multiple choice, short questions, and so on. If your department issues a syllabus then this will be a good guide. If a syllabus does not appear to be available then ask the head of your department for one.

Take a look at past examination papers, which are generally available from the library or your department, and compare the subjects covered from year to year. This will give you a clue as to what the examiners consider to be the most important topics. Together with advice from your lecturers you will have a good idea as to what you should study and what subjects to avoid. At the beginning of your first term you will probably be a little intimidated by the questions in the examination papers. But do not be put off by the fact that you do not understand the questions at this early stage.

As your examinations approach you will gradually see all your work falling into place and you will slowly gain a perspective view of your course. If you have studied properly, with a well organised timetable, revision should be quite effortless.

Universities are conspicuously devoid of students each spring! Thousands of heads are buried in text books and people are hurriedly cramming facts in an effort to learn everything which should have been covered earlier in the year.

If you have followed a flexible timetable, which allows you to revise your work at regular intervals, then the need for vast amounts of extra work at examination time will be reduced. You will need to readjust your timetable only to allow for more periods of revision. The need for learning new material should

not occur if you have studied steadily throughout the year. Following a study plan will make sure that you have learnt all the basic material well in advance of the examinations. You will be able to walk into the examination room with confidence.

As the exams approach, you should appraise your work and check the syllabus. Make sure that you have done all the work necessary and that nothing important has been overlooked. Immediately before your exams make sure that you are relaxed. Get a good night's sleep before — don't burn the midnight oil trying to cram a few more facts into your muddled mind. You should also be certain that you have all you need for the exam — pens, pencils, and so on. It is astounding to see the number of students who forget something vital.

When you arrive at your seat in the examination room, arrange your belongings so that you can get at them easily. Sort your desk out so that it is neat and tidy and sit back relaxed waiting for the word to begin.

Start the exam by carefully reading the set paper. Check the instructions — the number of students who answer the wrong number of questions is astonishing! Never rush to start writing your answers. Be calm and read the paper carefully. As with essay writing, make sure that you answer the questions as they are set. Do not get sidetracked into irrelevancies. Write legibly, as messy answers do not help the examiner and can only mean lower marks.

When you have finished writing, check your answers and once again make sure that the instructions at the beginning of the paper have been followed. This check should take place in the last few minutes of the exam. Never walk out early. Your answers will take up most of the time allotted and you should divide up your time fairly for the answers. Do not get carried away on one question and then find you only have half an hour left to write another three essays!

At the end of the examination hand in your paper and walk out ready to prepare for the next one. Avoid lengthy post mortems about the paper if you can. They do not help and only serve to shake your confidence.

The road to graduation ends at final examinations and you will not succeed in these exams unless you have studied throughout your university career. Follow a well structured timetable, and continually revise your work, and you will do well.

The road to exam success may well be a bumpy one from the aspect of studying but it certainly is nothing less than mountainous from all other angles.

The problems of just keeping yourself fit and happy seem to hit you every day. How to cook, where to buy good cheap clothes, how to do the washing and ironing, and all the other day to day chores which you probably haven't done before, are all regular problems which first year students meet.

The most recurrent moan of all students is their lack of money. This is usually because first year students have not had any experience of handling a budget, and quite often their first attempt fails. Do remember that student grants are not large amounts of money, even though your first grant cheque may seem a vast sum. But the spending power of most students is well below that of their friends who have a job.

4 Looking After Yourself

University College, Oxford

Many students do not qualify for a full grant from their local education authority. Parents and guardians are expected to contribute to the student's income to bring it to the level of a full grant. For some families, especially in times of economic recession, this is not possible and so many students have to make do with a lot less than a full grant.

If you do not receive a full grant and your parents are unable to give you any extra money you will probably need to supplement your income. If you decide to do this you must be certain that whatever you do to get extra cash will not interfere with your studies. It is far better to miss out on a few social events because you cannot afford them than to miss out on studies because you are working to pay for your leisure interests.

To supplement your grant you will probably need to find some form of casual employment. Whatever the job, make sure that it does not affect the level of your grant. The government sets the level of student earnings below which the grant is not affected.

This level changes from year to year, so check it before you start working. The leaflets about grants from your education authority will tell you what the level is for your particular year.

One of the most popular forms of student employment during termtime is as a member of the staff in any of the university bars. The pay is not that great but you do stand the chance of getting a lot of drinks bought for you! Local pubs will also offer casual employment to students and sometimes these pubs advertise in student newspapers.

Restaurants and clubs sometimes employ students as waiting staff or receptionists, and some students earn a fair amount of spare cash by running mobile discos. The types of casual employment vary from town to town, and a chat with second year students will give you an idea of what is available. Whatever you decide on, make sure that there is time to do it and include working hours in your timetable.

Some students may not have the time to work during term and will supplement their grant by taking on short term employment during vacations, especially in the summer. The types of jobs available in the summer are much more varied than during term time and there is often the chance to work abroad. Holiday jobs are explained in detail in chapter 8.

You may not need to earn extra cash, but you must be prepared to limit your spending in order to survive the year. Timetabling is important in ensuring the success of your studies but budgeting your spending is vital to the success of your money matters.

At the beginning of your first term you will receive what will look like a large amount of money, either from your local education authority, your parents, or both. But remember that this sum has to last for the entire term of about ten weeks. You have to pay your rent, buy food, books and clothes, and spend on social events, as well as saving enough cash for the fare home at the end of term. Another factor which is often overlooked is that your grant for the winter and spring terms includes some money which is supposed to be available to you during the vacation. This is described as the 'vacation element'. In theory, you are expected to be able to retain some of your grant at the end of these terms. In practice, this is not usually possible and most students spend these vacations drawing social security benefits (see chapter 8).

The few hundred pounds which you have available at the beginning of the term will dwindle, for many, into a bank overdraft. In other words you are spending money from a bank account which has nothing in it — effectively, borrowing money from your bank. This happens because spending is not budgeted properly and advice is not sought from the student account officer at the bank.

If you find that you are running out of money your bank manager will always be prepared to talk to you about the possibility of having an overdraft. But he is also the person who can help you avoid the necessity for one. He can help you budget your money, he can advise you about spending wisely and show you how to avoid overspending on insurance schemes, and he can offer a large range of financial services which will help to keep your account in credit.

At the beginning of your university career you will have opened a bank account. This will have been the current account which allows you to spend money using cheques as a means of payment. Banks are very keen on obtaining students' business. For example, the TSB offers students free banking while at college and for a year after. They usually back this with a cheque guarantee card and credit facilities. There is also preferential treatment if you apply for one of their mortgages later on.

Apart from the usual current account, all banks offer deposit facilities. Unlike current accounts, money on deposit accumulates interest. After some time the account will have more money in it than when it was opened. So deposit accounts, also called investment accounts, are used as a method of building up your savings. You do not receive a cheque book for such accounts and the bank may require some notice if you want to withdraw any of the money.

Whether you save money in a bank deposit account or not, you will still need a steady supply of cash for day to day expenses. You can withdraw cash from your current account by presenting a cheque at your own branch of your bank. However this may not always be convenient.

You can apply to your bank for a cheque guarantee card. This enables you to cash cheques up to £50 at any branch of any bank in the United Kingdom and in any bank abroad displaying the Eurocheque symbol which appears on all cheque cards. These cards will also guarantee payment of your cheques up to £50, so you can use the card when paying by cheque in shops, restaurants, and so on.

When you want to cash a cheque at a bank using your guarantee card you will naturally only be able to do so during normal banking hours, usually between 9.30am and 3.30pm. This may not always be convenient, although some banks may have a later evening opening, so you could apply for a cash card.

Cash cards can be inserted into the cash dispensing machines which are often found outside the larger branches. The card allows you to withdraw money from your current account without having to write a cheque and the dispensing machines may be used outside normal banking hours. There is a limit to the amount you can withdraw in any one day but it is usually sufficient to see you through your spending for quite some time.

Another method of being able to spend money without having any cash in your pocket is to have a credit card. The major British credit cards are Access, Barclaycard and Trustcard. You do not need to have an account with any particular bank to apply for these cards. You do, however, have to satisfy the bank issuing the card that you can afford the repayments. If you want a credit card you must complete an application form, which is on display in most banks. If your application is successful you will receive the card with a spending limit which must not be exceeded.

When you use a card to buy goods or services you are asked to sign a voucher as a record of the sale. The shop is paid immediately by the credit card company and you pay the credit card company either in a lump sum or by instalments. The minimum monthly payments are set at £5 or five per cent of the total owing, whichever is the greater.

Credit cards can also be used to obtain cash. VISA banks will allow you to draw cash against either Barclaycard or Trustcard, while banks affiliated to Access will allow cash against an Access card. The amount withdrawn will be debited to your credit card account together with a small handling charge.

Credit cards are a convenient method of paying for goods and services but it is possible to run up large bills which you may find difficult to pay off. Use a credit card wisely perhaps paying only for books or clothes. Don't use your credit card just on impulse as your credit card will attract interest each month if you do not pay your account in full.

An informal chat with your bank manager will help to sort out the type of bank accounts you should have and what type of financial services you need. Don't be scared or embarrassed about going to see the bank manager, or the student accounts officer; they are very approachable and know far more about student finances than you do.

The major drain on your finances will certainly be your rent. You can also expect to spend a rather large amount of your money on food. The rest will be spent on books, clothes, records and social events. Some students may also be able to run a car or motorcycle. Once you have paid your grant into your current account you should pay the rent — this is your number one priority, as you cannot study without somewhere to live. You may be able to pay your rent automatically each month by standing order — ask your bank.

For self-catering students, buying food will be a major drain on their money. For those students who are not in self-catering accommodation the payment for meals will be one of the most expensive items on their budget.

Shopping around for good cheap food will not be a waste of time. You will soon find out where to get cheap vegetables, good cuts of meat and reasonably priced provisions. Generally speaking, the larger supermarket chain stores are more competitively priced than the smaller corner stores — and, surprisingly, some campus shops. Also, fruit and vegetable markets which are held in most large towns each week are worthwhile visiting for cheap potatoes, carrots, sprouts, and so on.

Self-catering students will find that it often works out more economical if a small group clubs together to buy food. The members of the group can then share out the food, or cook meals together.

Remember also that it is generally cheaper to buy fresh vegetables than tinned or frozen food. It may not be convenient to prepare fresh vegetables, but in many instances they are more nutritious. There will, however, be limited cupboard space in your shared kitchen and so large sacks of potatoes are certainly not a good idea. It is sensible to work out a weekly menu and just buy the food needed for that. If you buy too much you will either run out of cupboard space or waste money by throwing away the food which goes off.

In addition to the problem of limited storage space, you will also have to face the fact that university cooking facilities are usually only basic. You will have to share your kitchen with a number of other students, all probably wanting to use the hotplates at the same time! It is not common to find student kitchens with a great array of cooking equipment. Usually, they contain a few electric rings or a small table top oven or two.

Popular meals in student kitchens include sausages or pies and boiled potatoes and so on. Chips feature high on the popularity ratings as they are quick and easy to cook. However, student mealtimes need not be so boring. There is an enormous range of meals you can cook with limited facilities and a few utensils.

Omelettes, salads, curries, stews and casseroles are all simple to prepare, easy to cook, and within the student budget. If you have not done any cooking before the following basic recipes will prove quite useful.

Omelettes:

2 eggs, butter, salt, pepper

Beat the eggs in a large mug and add salt and pepper. Melt a small amount of butter in a frying pan and add the egg mixture. Fry for about one minute and fold the omelette in half. Slide it out of the pan and it is ready to eat. Be careful not to use too much butter as the omelette will become greasy. Vary this recipe by adding small slices of cheese, tomatoes, bacon, or any vegetable.

Salads:

A basic salad needs lettuce, cucumber, tomatoes, celery, cress or watercress, beetroot.

Ham, corned beef, cheese, eggs, coleslaw, pilchards, or some other main item can be added. Salads are so quick and easy to prepare and fortunately, in a crowded kitchen, they do not need the use of a cooker.

Curry:

¼lb meat, fish, or chicken, 2 teaspoons curry powder, 2 onions, tomato paste, gravy powder or cube

Slice the onions and fry them for about five minutes. Add a squeeze of tomato paste. Dissolve the gravy cube, or two teaspoons of gravy powder, in about half a pint of water and stir this into the pan. Add the curry powder and the meat, which should be prepared by chopping into small chunks. Cook the mixture on low heat for about one hour. Serve the curry with boiled rice.

Stews:

½lb stewing steak, potatoes, onions, carrots, turnips (available from some supermarkets as 'stewpack vegetables'), mixed herbs, salt, pepper, gravy cube or powder

Cut the steak into small chunks and remove any fat. Wash and prepare the vegetables by cutting them into cubes. Place the meat and vegetables into a saucepan and stir in the gravy. Add herbs, salt, pepper, and bring to the boil. Cook on low heat, known as simmering for about two hours.

Casseroles:

These are similar to stews except that the mixture is cooked in a heat proof dish in an oven, for a slightly longer time. Chicken, liver, and so on, can also be casseroled. Prepare in the same way as a stew and cook in a medium hot oven for three hours.

Many students do not eat enough. They complain that preparing meals wastes time which could be spent studying. However, it is vital to eat a couple of well balanced meals each day. You cannot study well unless you are healthy, and students who survive on glucose tablets, black coffee and alcohol will suffer the consequences.

Another chore which many students dislike is the washing. While you were living at your home your mother probably threw all your dirty clothes into the automatic washing machine at night and the next morning there were clean clothes ready to wear again. At university there is no-one to do the washing and certainly not the luxury of an automatic washing machine.

For most students a weekly visit to the launderette is the answer. Most campus universities have their own launderette

(*above*) The fourteenth-century Wool House in Southampton now houses the city's Maritime Museum; (*below*) City Hall, Cardiff was built in 1904. The tower to the left is 200 feet high

The Holy Sepulchre Church in Cambridge dates from 1104 and is the oldest surviving round church in England

and many non-campus universities have one near to the halls of residence. However, you can cut down the amount of money spent at the launderette by using it only for larger items such as sheets, or jeans and jackets. Almost everything else can be washed by hand. A few items can be rinsed out each night and left to dry on the radiator.

Certain types of clothing require different methods of washing. The type of wash a particular garment needs is marked on the label inside with a standard code number, one of eight in the Fabric Care Guide Code. These are shown on the side of many packs of washing powder.

Ironing is not much of a problem these days, with the use of modern fabrics. Cotton shirts will need a quick run over with a hot iron but this is not necessary with nylon shirts if they are dried on a coat hanger. Do not bother to iron underclothes, or socks; sweatshirts rarely need attention if drip-dried. Jeans, or trousers, or skirts, will need ironing, but they will not be washed every few days. Most halls of residence provide irons for first year students.

Over the years you will add to your wardrobe of clothes. The stock outfit of most students is jeans and tee shirts but some smarter clothes will be needed for formal functions.

However, clothes can be quite expensive and so it is wise to buy them from those shops which offer discounts to students — usually between ten and twenty per cent off the marked price. The student union will be able to give you a list of all the local shops offering cheap goods and services.

In addition, a number of shops have joined the National Student Discount Scheme. This is operated by NUS Marketing, a company owned by the National Union of Students. Again, the student union office will be able to provide a discount card and a list of the shops which are involved in the scheme. They will also be able to provide details about other national discount schemes such as those involving travel and records. Great Stuff Records supplies records by mail order to suit all tastes, and is run by NUS Marketing.

The Student Rail Card is a valuable service offered by British Rail. The card can be obtained from your student union, and you will need a passport size photograph and enough money to pay for the card.

This card entitles students to cheap travel on single, return and

Awayday journeys, on Inter-City sleepers, and Sealink services to the Channel Islands, Ireland and the Isle of Wight. There is, however, a minimum fare below which you do not get a reduction, but a fifty per cent cut is allowed on all fares after 6pm on weekdays and at any time during weekends and bank holidays. If you have to travel by train between your residence and your department, or are likely to travel home to see parents or friends at regular intervals, then the Student Rail Card will pay for itself many times over.

Another valuable student service with competitive prices is Endsleigh Insurance Services. This is the only insurance company to get the backing of the National Union of Students and has offices at most universities. However, all banks offer a comprehensive range of insurance services, so a chat with your bank manager about the types of plans which are available will be worthwhile.

Your main need for insurance will be to protect personal possessions against theft or damage. You will be asked to pay a small amount of money, or premium, each year according to the value of your possessions. In return for paying this premium the insurance company will refund the value of any property that is stolen or damaged and the terms under which they will do this will be outlined in a written agreement, or policy. In addition to personal possessions policies, you can also obtain insurance for travel, health, cars, and your own life.

If you own a car then, by law, it must be insured. But running a car can be an expensive business, even though a few students seem to manage it. Most students who do decide to buy a car opt for small, middle aged family saloons. They may not be as flashy as a sports car, but they are generally quite economical to run.

When buying a car or motorcycle for the first time it is better to go to a dealer than to a private individual. Going to a dealer provides a greater amount of legal protection against any faults or inaccuracies in the sale.

The car should look as though it has been cared for. A heap, rattling with rust, is going to cost too much in repairs. It should also run smoothly — ask the dealer for a test drive before you buy. Have a look under the bonnet and check that everything is in good working order. If necessary, take a mechanically-minded friend with you so that you can get an honest, independent opinion of the state of the car.

After purchasing a car you will not be able to use it on the open road straight away. It must be taxed and insured and, if more than three years old, it must have a Ministry of Transport Test Certificate, or MOT. If you buy an old car, ask if it has a valid MOT certificate and for how long. If the car has no certificate then arrange for a roadworthiness test at a government approved garage. The vehicle excise duty must be paid and a 'Tax disc' displayed on the windscreen.

Your car must also be insured to protect it against damage or theft. The particular premium paid is according to the make and age of the car, together with a number of other factors. Your age will push up the premium. Young drivers are less experienced on the roads and therefore stand a higher risk of having an accident.

Once your car has passed an MOT test, and is taxed and insured, it can be used on the roads. However, trundling between your hall and your department can be an uneconomical way of using it. It is usually only necessary to drive on long journeys, so if you can walk then do so, as it will save money.

Keeping your car roadworthy is important to your own safety as well as that of other road users. The cost of repairs can be astronomical and if you can maintain your own car, or get a friend to do it, a significant amount of cash can be saved. If you need any spare parts go to a garage which offers student discount. Do not try and cut corners to save money. Car mascots are not necessary, but brakes are, so don't get your priorities mixed.

If you would like to learn to drive, apply to the Driver and Vehicle Licensing Centre at Swansea for a provisional licence. Application forms are available from Post Offices. With a provisional licence you can apply for lessons at a local driving school. Many of these offer student discounts, but make sure that lessons will fit between lectures. At some universities and polytechnics the local police offer courses in advanced driving techniques and also instruction for motorcycle riders. These courses are invaluable as they increase awareness about road safety.

Safety is seemingly lacking among students! They scale tall buildings during rag week, the scientists seem set on blowing up the campus, and some get so involved in a book that they might not notice that a carelessly thrown cigarette end has set the waste bin on fire. Minor accidents are certain to occur from time to time and so some idea of first aid will help, especially in communal kitchens.

Burns and scalds are common and should be treated by immersing the injured area in cold water. If a hand or an arm has been burned it is often easier to put the affected area beneath a running tap. Never use oils, butter, or creams, and never cover the burnt area with anything dirty or fluffy, such as a kitchen towel. If the burn is more than a couple of inches long it is a good idea to refer the sufferer to hospital.

Cuts are also common in student kitchens. Providing there is nothing embedded in the wound, the bleeding can be stopped by applying firm pressure directly to the injured area, which should be raised. If the gash is wide and it is difficult to stop the bleeding then stitches may well be needed and the patient should go to the local casualty unit.

Often, though, minor injuries can be dealt with at the university's health centre. These centres have doctors and nurses available to look after students and staff. Many universities have small sick bays which are open twenty-four hours a day for minor casualties and for the care of students too ill to look after themselves, but not quite ill enough to be admitted into hospital.

After arriving at university you will need to register as a patient of one of the doctors at the health centre. Your GP at home is no longer around to help. When registering, take along your NHS Medical Card, which you will have had since birth. If you are ever ill at home during vacations your family doctor will be able to treat you as a temporary resident.

Student health centres provide all the normal range of medical services but they also provide care with special emphasis for students. Often there are psychiatrists available to help with emotional problems, and the health centre also has student counsellors attached to it to help in such cases.

Counsellors will discuss, confidentially, personal problems, homesickness, emotional upsets, or difficulties with studies. Some university health centres have psycho-sexual clinics to help those students with sexual problems.

As well as these formal problem-solving methods, with expert staff on hand to help, many universities also have student-run problem 'clinics'. These are known as 'Nightline' in most places. Generally, a couple of students run a friendly office throughout the night. Other students can drop in to discuss in confidence any problems they might have. The Nightline 'clinics' also offer a Samaritans style service on the telephone.

Emotional troubles are not the only ones which the student health service has to cope with. The health centres offer advice on contraception and deal with worries about venereal disease. They also help with dental services and can arrange appointments at opticians. The health centre staff will continue with any treatment that you have been receiving from your GP, and they will look after the specific needs of anyone suffering from a handicap.

In order to do this, however, the health service must know about your medical background. At the start of the first term you will be asked to complete a questionnaire about your health record. These questionnaires, like all other medical matters, are completely confidential and are only open to discussion between patient and doctor.

While at university you may also have some legal difficulties. Sometimes students can overstep the mark in the pursuit of good fun, or will come into contact with the law as a result of some motoring offence. If the police are convinced that a crime has been committed, they can make an arrest on what is referred to as 'reasonable grounds of being guilty'. They must tell you directly that you have been arrested before a legal arrest has been performed.

After arrest you will be told your rights and cautioned. The arresting officer will tell you that anything you say will be written down and may be produced in evidence in court. It is often wise to remain silent until legal advice has been sought.

You are entitled to make a telephone call from the police station in order to get legal advice. If you are being questioned and no mention has been made of obtaining a solicitor, then demand to make a call to seek help. Generally, it is wise for students to telephone their student union president or welfare officer who will arrange legal representation. Legal costs will usually be borne by the student union, or the legal aid scheme.

If you are arrested without a warrant then you must be charged with an offence and brought before a magistrate within twenty-four hours of the arrest, or released on police bail. At weekends this time limit is extended to forty-eight hours.

If you are arrested with a warrant then you only have to appear before a magistrate as 'soon as possible'. One point to remember about a warrant — make sure it refers to you, not somebody else, and check whether or not it mentions bail.

You can be arrested without a warrant and if there are 'reasonable grounds' for suspecting an offence has been or will be, committed. You can be arrested for possessing an offensive weapon in a public place, and for refusing to take, or failing, a breathalyser test.

Naturally, your contact with the police may not be concerned with an arrest. The police are allowed to stop you and make a search if they suspect possession of illegal drugs, firearms, or stolen property. And, surprisingly, you can be searched on suspicion of possessing, or destroying, the eggs of protected birds. The police can also go through your pockets if they think you are a terrorist. Of course, if the officer's suspicions are confirmed for any of these instances he will probably arrest you. He may also make an arrest if you refuse to be searched, because you could be seen to be obstructing a police officer in the execution of his duty.

If any legal problems arise, seek help through your student union, which will be able to get you a solicitor. The Citizens Advice Bureau will also help in legal matters by telling you which solicitors are members of the legal aid scheme. Students are entitled to legal aid in criminal and civil proceedings. You will also be entitled to some help under the Green Form Scheme. This scheme is for those people who just want legal advice, and is available up to the value of £25.

One common reason for students to seek legal advice is a problem with accommodation, or a landlord. Any problems associated with accommodation should be discussed with whoever owns the property and expert advice sought from the university accommodation officer.

As a general guide, note that if you are renting accommodation and are paying in weekly or monthly sums you are entitled to a rent book. This should stipulate the terms and conditions of the renting and should also record all payments. If you pay in instalments greater than one month, then demand a receipt. These longer term rentals are called 'Tenancy Agreements'. You cannot get out of these agreements until the period of the tenancy has expired. So if your personal circumstances change you will still have to pay the rent for the agreed period.

If you think you are paying too much for accommodation then

take the matter up with the Rent Officer at the local Town Hall. If you live in furnished accommodation where the landlord lives on the premises then you can take your complaints to the Rent Tribunal. These offices might find that you are eligible for a rent rebate and they will arrange for the rent to be reduced. Don't be put off going to these offices, they cannot increase your rent!

If you face eviction then seek advice from the student union, the university accommodation officer and the Rent Officer. It is difficult for landlords to evict tenants of rented accommodation and in every instance they must get a court order to do so.

If you do get any problems like these, or difficulties with studies, health, or sexual matters, then make sure that you seek help and advice. Also get help with insurance, money matters, and any of the day to day things that might need a bit of organising. There is no need to let them spoil your academic career.

One of the biggest attractions of university life is the great potential for varied social activities. It is often true, also, that your social life is as important as your studies. You will not be able to study properly without being relaxed and free from any worries. A restricted social life could well lead to unhappiness and, consequently, studies will suffer.

For many students social life revolves round the union bar. At non-campus universities a large pub is often the social centre. There are occasionally bars in common rooms, halls of residence and other university buildings such as sports halls. In the first few weeks of their university careers, and after exams, some students tend to get rather carried away and consume large amounts of alcohol. However, despite these occasional outbursts, most students are not alcoholics but just social drinkers, having a few drinks for an hour or so each evening.

Generally, bars in universities offer all the normal range of services found in public houses. However, the range of beers available at university bars is usually larger than that in pubs and mostly the prices are also lower.

Union bars tend to be male dominated. It is most likely that this emphasis is an inevitable by-product of the male dominance of universities generally. It follows therefore that the activities in union bars are also male dominated. There are table football games, pinball machines, snooker tables, pool tables and so on.

In addition to these pastimes most unions offer some form of organised entertainment on most evenings.

5 Social Life

Charles Rennie Mackintosh Library —
Glasgow School of Art

Usually these are discos or musical concerts, or pop concerts. They are generally quite cheap and often the bar is open for longer than the normal licensing hours, as a result of a 'bar extension'. Because of the attraction of drinking for long hours, and the relative freedom of university life, there are always some students who drink too much. Fortunately, they are rare.

There is only one cure for a hangover, and that is to avoid alcohol. But this is unlikely for most students and so you will probably spend a few unhappy hours vowing 'never again'.

The dreadful feeling of pain and sickness which you might get on the morning after a bout of drinking is due to the additives in alcoholic drinks. These additives are known collectively as 'congeners'. Bad hangovers can be avoided by choosing drinks that have few congeners. Vodka and gin are low congener drinks, but strong beer, red wine and brandy are high in congeners. It is more difficult than it seems to avoid hangovers by not drinking too much, because once you have had a few drinks you are much more relaxed and it is difficult to say no to some more.

Part of a 'hungover' feeling is due to the dehydration associated with heavy drinking, so a few glasses of water as soon as you wake up will help. However, drinking some water before you go to sleep after a session in the bar will reduce the effects of dehydration and dilute the congeners.

One often quoted method of curing a hangover is receiving support from scientists. Honey and lemon juice provide an ample quantity of vitamin C which speeds up the breakdown of congeners. If you can take a drink which contains a lot of vitamin C before going to sleep then your hangover will be less drastic.

Naturally, to need a hangover cure you need to drink a lot. But what should you drink when there is such a large range of alcoholic beverages, and when you are unlikely to have been a regular visitor to public houses?

Beer in its various forms is probably one of the most widely consumed of all alcohols. This is a mixture of barley malt, hops, yeast and sugar. It is available as keg beer, from 'the wood', or in bottles. Most students prefer beer from the wood. This means it is pumped from barrels, traditionally wooden but now more usually metal, and, unlike keg beer, has no added gasses. Bottled beer also has added carbon dioxide.

Pale ale is a bottled beer and is usually stronger than the bottled light ale. Brown ale is the bottled form of mild, a dark, sweet beer, not as strong as bitter. Stout is a very dark bottled beer and has a sharp taste. There are some very strong beers. These 'real ales' are in great demand as a result of the Campaign for Real Ale (CAMRA).

Lager is often drunk by students, despite the fact that it is more expensive than beer. It is brewed for longer than bitter and consequently contains more calories and more alcohol. It is more gassy than bitter and you will probably not be able to drink large quantities.

One of the most popular 'short' drinks is gin. This is a grain spirit flavoured with juniper berries. It is served in single measures of one-sixth of a gill and is usually mixed with tonic water, although it can be mixed with water, lime juice, and bitter lemon.

Vodka has very little flavour and is generally produced from potatoes. It can be drunk with lime juice, tonic water and some branded mixers which are flavoured with peach juice. A 'Bloody Mary' is vodka mixed with tomato juice and a 'Screwdriver' is vodka with orange juice.

Rum is a spirit obtained by distilling molasses or sugar cane syrup. The sugar cane rum is clear and is called white rum, as opposed to the dark brown rum produced from molasses. White rum is often referred to as bacardi, which really is the brand name of one type of white rum. Both types of rum can be drunk with Coca-Cola.

The range of whiskies is enormous. Generally there are two types of Scotch whisky — grain and malt. Malt is the most popular and is distilled from barley. Grain whisky is made from maize and is blended to produce different tastes. There are also Irish whiskies, rye whiskies from America, Canadian whiskies and Bourbon. Most whisky is drunk with water, soda water, or ginger ale.

Alcoholic drinks for consumption on the premises of a licensed building can be bought only during normal hours or until the extension of hours has expired. Drinking must finish within ten minutes of the bar closing. You can be fined £100 if caught drinking after time. However, drinking-up time does not mean that you have to leave the building. You can stay there as long as you like, or until the landlord asks you to leave.

You can be arrested if you are suspected of being guilty of drunkenness or for being drunk and disorderly. There are also other offences which could arise, such as causing a public nuisance or, on occasions, indecency.

Of course, when driving a car or riding a motorcycle you should avoid taking alcohol. Your blood must not have more than 80mg of alcohol in each 100ml to remain within the law. As a *rough* guide you can take this to mean three measures of spirits or three half pints of beer. However, everyone reacts differently to alcohol and to avoid the risks of drunken driving it is wise not to drink at all.

Avoiding alcoholism is also important. It is estimated that drinking four pints, or equivalent, every day involves a high risk of dependence upon alcohol. If you find that you cannot stop drinking then contact Alcoholics Anonymous, a confidential organisation which deals with such problems.

Most of your social life will, however, be quite sober. You will probably have a few drinks with friends each week. Every so often, though, there may be an invitation to a party or disco.

Student parties have an undeserved reputation for being wildly uninhibited. This type of party is far more the exception than the rule. Most of them are small gatherings of people in common rooms. Everyone takes along a bottle of wine or some cans of beer and they all chat and dance the night away with a paper cup of drink. However it is at student parties that you may be introduced to drugs. Drugs are not socially or legally accepted forms of stimulant and consequently you should take care if any are offered.

Drugs are grouped as 'soft' and 'hard' which implies that soft drugs are not dangerous. But they are just as easy to become addicted to. Whatever the type of drug, once 'hooked' it is hard to stop taking it. Indeed, most drug addicts are likely to be taking soft varieties as the hard drugs are very difficult to obtain.

The hard drugs include heroin and morphine, both of which are based on opium which is extracted from poppy seeds. It is illegal to possess these drugs, unless you are a registered addict or have a medical, or pharmaceutical, qualification.

The more readily available soft drugs are also illegal to possess for anyone other than those medically qualified. These drugs include barbiturates, amphetamines and tranquillisers. The barbiturates will probably be introduced to you as 'barbs'. They are also sometimes referred to as 'downers'. These pills have sedative effects and can sometimes be hypnotic. Amphetamines will be referred to as 'speed'. They are so called because they accelerate the body's activities. These pills are occasionally referred to as 'uppers' or 'eye openers'. The tranquillisers include Valium and Librium.

Another soft drug is cannabis. This is referred to as 'grass', 'hash', 'pot', or 'weed'. It is usually smoked in combination with small amounts of tobacco in self-rolled cigarettes. Doctors say that this soft drug leads to addiction to hard drugs. It is illegal to possess or grow cannabis.

If you are involved in taking drugs and want to stop, or find that you are addicted, then get help. Go and see your doctor, who will probably refer you to a Drug Dependency Unit. The doctor will not ask where you get your drugs from or who supplies them. Even if he does find out, his commitment to patient confidentiality will ensure that you do not get tangled up in legal problems.

A serious offence is possession with intent to supply any drug to others. Penalties range from probation care to fines and long term imprisonment. Drugs are made available from a local dealer, called a 'pusher'. He sells various drugs, or occasionally just one particular brand, usually at high prices. The pusher will rarely approach new students. They will be introduced to him by a student who buys drugs regularly.

Some people, rightly or wrongly, associate drugs with pop concerts. Most universities have well organised concerts from major recording artists, usually about once each week. These are arranged by the Entertainments Committee, or 'Ents' as they are called. In addition to pop concerts, or 'gigs', they organise a whole range of social events such as discos. The record industry considers the university gigs important. Consequently you will be able to see a number of well known bands as well as other less famous, and amateur, bands.

If you have never been to a gig before, make sure that you stand at the back of the hall. The amplification is enormous and occasionally can be deafening. Don't stand too close to the loudspeakers as the noise could permanently damage you hearing. Even if you keep away from the speakers your ears may whistle during the day after the concert. If the problem doesn't clear up by the next day then see your doctor as soon as possible.

Like most university social activities, discos are male dominated. The men tend to drink together in small groups around the edge of the dance floor in the hope of seeing a woman they would like to dance with. Usually it is the women in the disco who venture out on to the dance floor to begin with and for many it is a daunting experience. If you do not like this then avoid dancing in the early part of the evening. Waiting until the dance floor is reasonably packed will help those who are self-conscious.

Unless they have a permanent boyfriend, women can be plagued with requests to venture out on to the dark floor for a dance. It is usually this way round, although occasionally some women do ask men for a dance. If you do not want to dance with someone then say so. There is no point in getting into a situation that you would rather avoid!

Most discos at universities are casual affairs and often the disc jockey is a student working to supplement his grant. However, you will find some more 'up-market' discos in the town where casual clothes are out and smartness is in. These discos, and

night-clubs are more expensive than university discos and the bar prices are much higher as well, so you are not likely to be able to afford many trips.

Nightclubs are not the only form of entertainment in the town. There are cinemas, theatres, sports centres, restaurants, civic centres, concert halls, and so on. Many of these places will offer student discounts, so check this out before going.

Another matter to check before going out is the time of the last bus or train back to the campus or to your hall. Of course, you may be living in the town itself and can quite easily walk home. But many students will live some way from the town and could face a long, dark and lonely walk, or an expensive taxi fare.

Living outside the town should not preclude students from taking part in its activities, even though some campus universities, especially, are rather isolated. Most university towns have a lot to offer students — casual jobs, holiday employment, pubs, cheap entertainment, and a wide range of discount shops. Of course, in many instances a university, such as Oxford, is part of the town and the local events are organised by the university authorities.

Much of your social life will be spent in the various activities of university clubs and societies. There are all sorts of sports clubs from rugby, netball, and hockey, to karate, trampolining and sub-aqua diving. There are cultural societies ranging from operatics to Winnie the Pooh Fan Clubs, and political groups from the extreme left to the extreme right. There are general leisure clubs which cover such things as train spotting and painting, and of course there are departmental societies and clubs for the various ethnic groups and religious beliefs. But if there isn't a club to represent your interest there is virtually nothing stopping you from forming one. Of course, you will have to apply for the necessary permission, and the activities must be legal.

As you become more involved with your favourite pastime you will probably take part in the organisation of the relevant club, possibly becoming a committee member. Committees are responsible for the running of almost everything at universities. How well the various committees function depends upon the people who form them. If the individuals are not interested in their post then the committee is unlikely to do a good job and the club will suffer.

The sixteenth-century Old Mol's House in Exeter was formerly a coffee house. The adjacent fifteenth-century St Martin's Church retains its original oak barrel-vaulted roof

Tom Tower, Christ Church College, Oxford was started during the reign of Henry VIII and later completed by Sir Christopher Wren

All committees run along slightly differing lines, but the basic principles of operation are the same. If you apply for a post you will be asked to address a committee meeting and explain why you want to take on the job. The members will then ask you some questions and decide in private whether or not to award you the post. If you are elected to the committee in this way you will have to abide by the rules of a written constitution.

A constitution is a rule book by which the club and its committee are governed. It will outline the aims of the club and set out how the committee shall operate. It will also dictate the functions of the various committee posts and outline the disciplinary action available to tackle members of the club who break the rules.

The most senior committee post is that of chairman, and new club members are not likely to be elected to it for some time. The chairman is responsible for the arrangement and organisation of committee meetings, making sure the discussion flows and that the constitution is adhered to. He will also be called upon to advise the committee and to interpret constitutional matters. Generally, chairmen are not allowed to vote in committee meetings. They are supposed to be impartial in their control of the meeting, and for this reason an experienced member of the club is chosen for the post.

Secretaries of committees are invaluable. They are the backbone of the club and are very hard workers. The secretary is responsible for most of the administration of the committee and usually for the club as a whole. He prepares agendas for meetings and takes down the minutes — a written record of what occurs in committee. It is often his job to write the club's letters and to make any necessary telephone calls. In one sense the secretary is the link between the club and the rest of the university.

The treasurer has the task of looking after the money and making sure that the club does not spend so much that it needs an overdraft. He has to maintain the accounts, look after the budgets and arrange fund raising activities.

These are the three main committee posts common to all clubs and societies. But each club differs as to the basis of the rest of the committee and your club might have such posts as a publicity officer, a university liaison officer, or just general committee members.

How to behave in committee meetings is something you will

learn as you attend more of them. The first thing to remember if you are elected to a committee is to do the job as described in the constitution. In the meeting itself, never interrupt other members' speeches but wait until the chairman asks you to speak. If the rest of the committee disagrees with your opinion don't get upset and rush out of the room disgusted. That will only give a bad impression to the committee and the other members probably will not listen to your opinion in the future.

Talking in committee meetings may well be your first taste of serious debate, but your university is certain to provide endless opportunities for discussion, debate and general public speaking. For final year students, and others who have had experience of speaking in public, it can seem quite easy. But, if you have never done it before, it can be a quite daunting prospect to stand up in front of a few hundred people and tell them that they are wrong about some matter.

At public debates a motion is presented to the meeting by the chairman, who will introduce two speakers, one in favour of it and one against. Naturally, these speakers will have been told in advance what the motion is, so that they can prepare their speeches. The speakers are then allotted a certain time in which to convince the audience of their points of view. After both speeches have been heard, and any questions from the audience answered, the chairman will ask for a show of hands in favour of each speaker. The motion will then be declared as lost or won.

Speaking in debate is not really different from any other form of public speaking. The first rule to remember is to make sure that the audience can hear you — many people mumble, or speak too quickly. Speak at normal conversational speed and always have a good idea of what you intend saying. If necessary, write your speech down but, like presenting a paper in a seminar, never read this out as it will sound boring. It is a good idea just to jot down the main points to use as a reminder.

When speaking in public make sure that you look at individual members of the audience. Personalise your speech as much as possible because this will help the audience to identify with you and will strengthen your argument. Also try to entertain the audience. A funny line or a joke or two will help to create a good impression.

Some of the greatest opportunities for public speaking occur during university rag weeks. These are the few days of light relief when anything and everything occurs! There are 'Master-mind' contests at one extreme and custard pie throwing championships at the other, but rag weeks do have a much more serious aspect. All the events are sponsored, or raise money in some other way, for charity. In fact university rag weeks are major contributors to charity organisations.

Getting involved with Rag Week is quite easy. Just go along to one of the committee meetings and tell the organisers what you want to do. If money can be raised from it they will probably agree. Nothing is too eccentric for Rag Week. But many of the events are races of one kind or another, so it is usually the sporting students who win the prizes.

Sport is a very important aspect of student social life. It has been estimated that two thirds of all students are involved in some form of sporting activity, whether as members of an organised team or as casual users of the various facilities.

The sporting facilities at most universities are first class. They are usually well looked after by expert staff and provide for almost every sport imaginable. If the university cannot provide the facilities it often comes to an arrangement with the local authority, or some other body.

Most sports clubs at universities are run along very strict lines. No stragglers are allowed to play in the teams and training sessions are held on several evenings each week. Selection is highly competitive with only the top players being allowed to play for the first team.

The reason for this intense competition is that university teams compete in high class national competitions as well as local matches. High level inter-university matches are organised by the University Athletic Union (UAU), for men's team games, and by the Women's Inter Varsity Athletics Board (WIVAB). The less important, non-championship games are usually organised at an individual club level.

At the beginning of each academic year the various sports clubs hold trials for everyone interested in playing a particular game. The senior members of the club will decide on the level of individual ability and allocate places in the relevant teams. The club organisers will monitor a player's progress through the year and transfer up or down according to performance.

If you do not want to play organised sport, there is still a vast range of facilities. Normally, there are squash courts, swimming pools, tennis courts, and so on, for use by individuals who are not necessarily members of the relevant society. In addition to these individual sports and the high level team sports you can also play for your department or your hall. These games tend to be taken less seriously than those organised by specific clubs.

Getting involved in some form of sporting activity is a good way of keeping fit. Fitness and health are valuable in working towards exam success. If you do not want to involve yourself in sport, then an occasional brisk walk will be worthwhile.

For some students a pleasant walk on a Sunday with a few friends is a good addition to their social life. It will also help them to relax and forget the rigours of study for a few hours. The Sunday walk is often taken after morning service in church; many students are faithfully religious and the relevant societies and churches often form the basis of their social life.

Although the majority of British students will be Anglicans, Roman Catholics, or non-conformist Christians, there are many other religious groups, which are catered for at universities. There will probably be groups for Quakers, Jews, Moslems, Sikhs, and Buddhists, to name just a few.

You will certainly find that your university or college has chaplains to represent the Anglican and Roman Catholic faiths. You may also find representative ministers from local Methodist churches, the United Reformed Church, or the Salvation Army. All of them are available for discussions about religious matters and, in addition, they can help with personal problems. The chaplains are also responsible for organising a number of social events. They run coffee mornings, cheese and wine evenings and debates, as well as the religious services. They take an interest in many of the activities organised by the student union and can often be spotted in the union bar or in common rooms.

Whether you become involved in religion, sport, clubs and societies, or just go to the bar every night, your studies naturally must not suffer because of your social activities. It will be very difficult to turn down the mass of invitations to attend various social events. If you say that you are staying in to write an essay you may be derided for being boring or a bookworm, but you will have to learn to put up with any ridicule.

The important point to remember is to balance your social life and your studies. If you spend all of your time studying you will be short of friends and could well be unhappy. Your mind will also become so clogged that you will run out of fresh ideas, which will be a serious disadvantage when it comes to exams. Conversely, too much time spent socialising will jeopardise your work and ruin your budget. The rough rule is to spend about half of your free time studying and leave the remaining half available for taking part in the university's rich social life.

6 Love and Physical Relationships

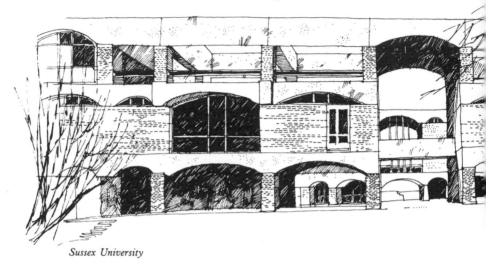

Sussex University

During Introduction Week you will probably be given all sorts of information about contraception, and told where to get help with such problems as pregnancy or venereal disease. It is all sound medical advice but it can create the wrong impression. Often, there is no real appreciation of relationships and love is rarely mentioned. Yet it is precisely in these areas where most first year students need advice.

On arriving at university or polytechnic, at eighteen years old, you may feel mature enough to cope with intense relationships with the opposite sex but, despite this, your youthful age ensures that you are relatively inexperienced in handling such situations. Indeed, even for older couples there are problems and one of the most recurrent is difficulty with a sexual relationship. Part of this is due to the lack of immediate parental advice. If you do have problems then you often have to solve them alone.

Most students will have had some form of friendship with members of the opposite sex — many of them arrive at university with a boyfriend or girlfriend from home to help them move in. After parting, the couple eagerly await the end of term so that they can be together again. It is, however, quite common for

such relationships to come to an end during the first term. This is probably because it is difficult to maintain a friendship when the partners are separated for long periods.

It is also very common for couples to meet in the first few weeks at university and to form a relationship which lasts for years. Many such couples get married soon after they have graduated. Other students have a number of partners throughout their stay at university and some never form a stable relationship at all.

The subject of sexual involvement is so complex and varied that, though it is easy for the university authorities to dispense information about contraception and so on, it is difficult for them to advise about individual personal problems. These are left to be discussed at an individual level. However, it is because of this attitude that many students find their studies are suffering. They may have some problem which they think they can sort out themselves but for which they really need help.

More advice is needed about emotional difficulties than about contraception and venereal disease. You may want to end a relationship you can no longer cope with, or to form one with a new partner. You might want to patch up a rift caused by endless rows or you might be in love with more than one person. It is wise to get these problems sorted out as soon as possible.

If you already have a stable relationship and find that things are not running smoothly then it is vital to discuss the situation with your partner. Pretending that the problem will go away if you ignore it will only aggravate the situation. If your partner is at home then any problems can get exaggerated because you are separated.

Some emotional troubles can probably be resolved by making some form of compromise. You may decide to end the relationship altogether, but if you seem unable to make a decision then seek advice. Talk to a close friend, to your parents, to your personal tutor, or to one of the counsellors, doctors, or psychiatrists at the health centre. In most cases, whoever you ask for help will not tell you exactly what to do. The adviser is more likely to listen to your story and then talk to you about the alternative courses of action available.

If you do decide to end the relationship then this could certainly affect your studies. You may find it difficult to work and will mope around, quite bored, missing the activities you were both involved in. Although it will be hard, try to alleviate the boredom and the feeling of rejection by packing so much into the day that there is no time to reminisce. Go out with friends, join new clubs and societies, and, most important, immerse yourself in academic work. Gradually you will adjust and be able to catch up on the work that you will almost certainly have missed out.

One of the most distressing experiences faced by some students is a relationship break-up just before examinations. This can result in missing out important revision because of unhappiness and worry. You must, despite everything, work very hard in an attempt to forget the problem. Tell your personal tutor or head of department about the situation, however difficult this may be. These people might be able to make some allowances when your exam papers are marked. If they cannot do that they will certainly help you to concentrate on your revision.

However, serious problems of this nature are fortunately quite rare and it is unlikely that you will encounter them. In fact, your main problem may well be finding a suitable partner of the opposite sex. Those people who worry about not being able to form a lasting relationship are probably those who are least likely to do so. They spend so much time worrying that they do not see possible partners approaching them! Certainly if you want to find a partner then go out and look for one, but do not get worked up about it. You will begin to feel inadequate if you are not successful. If worrying about it gets out of proportion, then seek some counselling advice.

The advice that is available will apply whether or not you are heterosexual or homosexual. Estimates vary as to the incidence of homosexuality, but it is generally agreed that around one in every thirty people is physically attracted to members of the same sex; despite society's rejection of homosexual men and women, and the consequent misconceptions about their lifestyle it is accepted without doubt that these people experience emotions similar to those of their heterosexual friends. Homosexuals do fall in love and they have the same sort of relationship problems as heterosexuals. If you are homosexual do not think that the student counsellors are unable to help you. They will give you the same confidential service that they give to all students.

One problem which might arise is the belief that you are becoming homosexual. This is not unusual and there is no need to think that you are 'turning queer'. It is very common for people to go through a phase in their development when they are attracted to members of the same sex. This happens most among people in their mid-teens, although it sometimes occurs in older people. If you think that you are becoming sexually attracted to members of your own sex then your studies may suffer. You will be concerned that you are not 'normal' and at the prospect of being labelled 'gay'. If this happens, then seek advice. Your doctor, or the student counsellor, or the university 'gay' society will all have handled such problems many times before and will not be embarrassed to offer confidential assistance. If you want some anonymous advice then contact one of the many 'Gay Switchboards' which offer a Samaritan style service. The number of your nearest Switchboard will be in the directory, although the twenty-four hour London Switchboard will help anyone.

Despite the picture painted so far, most students will probably have a happy time and be able to resolve the occasional problems that are bound to occur. When you arrive at university you will probably be sexually inexperienced. There are no figures available, but it has been suggested that less than fifty per cent of male first years and less than thirty per cent of female first years have had sexual intercourse before they start university. The rest, the majority, are virgins, and their first experience of sexual intercourse may occur during their three years at university.

Some people do not want any sexual activity until they are married, and if you have this point of view then you are entitled to protect it. If you wish to remain a virgin during your time at university you may want some form of outlet for sexual tension and emotion. Indeed those students who are not virgins will also want some release for their sexual feelings.

There have been a number of studies of human sexual behaviour but the Kinsey Report is the most famous. This was a large scale research project performed in America in the 1950s. The study showed that most men under the age of thirty have some form of sexual 'outlet', on average, twice each week, although the number of outlets each day varied from none to more than one. The figures for women are estimated by Kinsey as being much lower than for men. He claims that the sexual drive in women is much lower than in men and so they have less need for an outlet for their sexual energies. By 'outlet' Kinsey means any form of sexual satisfaction.

The peak of the male sex drive occurs in the late teens and early twenties — the age group of most students. Females, however, reach their peak of sexual drive later than men. It is accepted that the female peak sex drive occurs in their mid to late twenties. At university, therefore, there is a difference between men and women in the need for a sexual outlet. In addition, because there are far more men students than women, the men tend to become frustrated and eager to grasp almost any opportunity for sexual experience.

This can often be the cause of problems. The male partner can be too interested in the sexual side of the relationship whereas the female partner can sometimes seem decidedly uninterested in sexual intercourse. It is a seemingly common problem and can be resolved only by discussion and advice. Because of these occasional difficulties, and because of their high sex drive, men will often opt for casual sex with a woman who they have met only recently, the 'one night stand' or, occasionally, a rather understanding friend.

One of the most important things to remember is that unprotected sexual intercourse in young people, who are usually highly fertile, carries a strong risk of conception. You could find yourself at a very inappropriate time of your life facing parenthood or difficult decisions regarding abortion.

Apart from the risk of conception, casual sex with a number of different partners also increases the chances of picking up sexually transmitted diseases in both male and female. Worse still, it greatly increases the risk of cervical cancer in young women. Although in the past regular cervical cancer smear tests have been recommended for those aged over thirty-five, recent figures have confirmed a growing incidence of the disease in young women, linked to greater sexual freedom. So *all* sexually active women should insist on these regular painless tests which detect the problem at what is called the pre-cancer stage, when it is one hundred per cent curable. Your own GP, student health centre, Family Planning Clinic, and in some areas special Mobile Caravans, all offer this free test.

It is natural that young people in love, and especially perhaps young women within a seemingly stable relationship, should have a strong biological urge to start a child. But the harsh facts have to be faced. During university years or while studying on a grant parenthood is next to impossible from the financial angle, very unfair to the child and puts tremendous strain on both parents and on their ability to cope with studies and exams. If, however, you decide that you really do want children while at university you must seek early advice. Talk to your parents, your doctor and, if necessary, to the counsellors.

There are a number of different forms of contraception available for use by men or women. None of the methods is one hundred per cent effective, although some are much safer than others and, used correctly, the most widely accepted methods are fairly reliable. Nearly all are available under the NHS.

You will hear some forms of contraception referred to as 'barrier methods'. Barrier contraception is precisely that — a barrier which prevents sperm from the man entering the uterus, or womb, and combining with an ovum, or egg. Pregnancy occurs when one sperm joins together with an ovum in the upper part of the uterus known as the Fallopian tube. In the three or four millilitres of semen ejaculated by a man during intercourse there are about 300 million sperm.

The most frequently used form of barrier contraception, and the most effective, is the condom, or sheath. This is a small sealed tube of rubber which can be rolled over the erect penis. On ejaculation the semen remains in the sheath. When a sheath is used it should be put on carefully before any sexual contact occurs. This is important, as some sperm may be present in or on the penis before ejaculation and it takes only one sperm to cause pregnancy. An advantage of using a sheath is that it may help to prevent the transmission of sexual disease. Sheaths still do not come into the free family planning programme but they are quite cheap and can be bought at most chemist shops, or from vending machines in lavatories. They can also be obtained from barbers and hairdressers, as well as from mail order suppliers who advertise in the national press.

The female barrier method is the cap, or diaphragm. Cervical caps are available only on prescription and in the first instance, to ensure the right size and a good fit, the cap must be inserted round the head of the cervix by a doctor or family planning specialist. The woman then learns to insert it herself and this should be practised a few times before intercourse, as if it is put in the wrong place its contraceptive effect is lost. The cap should be used in conjunction with a spermicide — a jelly or foam which contains chemicals hostile to sperm — as this increases its effectiveness. Never use a spermicide alone; always use it with some other form of contraception, as the jelly is not totally effective. A cap should be left in place for at least six hours after intercourse as there may be sperm in the vagina which could reach the uterus if the cap is removed prematurely. It is necessary to visit a doctor at regular intervals so that the cap can be checked for correct functioning. If the cap regularly becomes dislodged it is not performing effectively and an alternative method of contraception should be considered.

Undoubtedly the most effective form of contraception is the Pill. In fact there are around thirty different brands of oral contraceptive Pill. The most usual type, the combined Pill, contains chemical preparations of the female hormones — oestrogen and progestogen (which occurs naturally as progesterone). By artificially raising the levels of these hormones in the body to the higher levels present in pregnancy, ovulation is prevented just as it is with a real pregnancy. The failure rate on this combined Pill is only one quarter of one per cent, provided it is taken regularly.

If by mistake a dose is missed, two pills should be taken the next day.

A great deal has been written about the dangers of the Pill, but a survey carried out over a six year period and involving some 46,000 women concluded that the risk of serious illness associated with the oral contraceptive was very small and that women may even be healthier when using it. However, a slightly greater possibility of thrombosis occurring has been confirmed. This is dosage related and is still far smaller than the risk of thrombosis in pregnancy. The only exception is for the older woman who may also be a heavy smoker.

The studies were largely carried out when high dosage Pills were in use. Since then the amounts of hormones contained in the Pill have been reduced and low dosage Pills, with a thirty per cent lower hormone content, have been produced. These are now widely prescribed and are especially applicable to older women and/or heavy smokers.

While obviously you must take your doctor's advice, it is helpful sometimes to remember also that there are many benefits from oral contraception. Apart from the fact that it requires no privacy to use, it also regulates periods and even reduces menstrual loss and pain. Bleeding occurs during the week when hormone levels are allowed to drop and this cyclic pattern is deliberately planned to simulate natural menstrual periods.

It is important to remember that the Pill does not confer protection immediately. There must be time for the hormone levels to be raised and your doctor will advise you about this. Side effects in just a few women can include breast tenderness and nausea in the first cycle, rather as in a real pregnancy, but this usually disappears. Some susceptible women find oral contraception induces a form of migraine headache and a few suffer from depression, which can often be relieved by use of pyridoxine, vitamin B6.

There is one type of Pill, known as the Mini Pill, which contains no oestrogen and relies for its contraceptive action on the other female hormone, progesterone. The more correct name is the progestogen-only Pill and, although the failure rate is somewhat higher, it is valuable for women who fear the thrombosis risk associated with the combined Pill or for whom oestrogen is contra-indicated because of varicose veins, high blood pressure, or other medical reasons. There is a tendency to irregular periods and some spotting in about twenty per cent of women using this type of oral contraception, but this will usually be tolerated if they are reassured. It is particularly important with the progestogen-only Pill to take it regularly. Even missing one day can result in pregnancy.

Finally, modern contraception offers a wide choice of what are called Intra Uterine Devices, or IUDs. Intra Uterine simply means inside the womb and that is where the small loop or coil is placed. Once made of plastic, the most popular devices now also contain copper and the latest and most comfortable shape for insertion is the Copper 7 or Copper T. Because the copper itself exerts a contraceptive effect, the devices of this kind can be smaller. Experts believe, and studies seem to confirm, that IUDs work in several ways. The copper content is directly hostile to sperm but the presence of the device also alters the mucus in the womb making it more difficult for the sperm to reach the egg and changing the nature of secretions so that any fertilised eggs cannot implant in the wall for further growth.

For the woman who has not had a child, the fitting of an IUD, which of course must be done by a GP or family planning expert, may involve some discomfort. After the fitting there may be cramp-like pains, similar to those associated with a period, but these do not usually last very long. A specially small device, known as the Mini-Gravigard, has been designed for women who have had no children or who have small wombs.

The IUD can be removed quite simply but this must always be done by a doctor. Occasionally the device may work out and a check should be kept by feeling for the special thread attached which confirms the presence of the IUD. The failure rate with IUDs is very low — only three per cent — but the device must be removed at once if a pregnancy occurs. Some cases of pelvic inflammation have been reported, but the latest and smaller types of device are proving more trouble free.

There are two ways to avoid pregnancy if using artificial means of contraception is found unacceptable or is irreconcilable with religious convictions. Both these methods are unreliable, even if followed scrupulously.

The first method is called the rhythm method. It is based on avoiding intercourse on the days when the woman is calculated to be at her most fertile. Ovulation usually takes place thirteen to fifteen days before the first day of the next period and sperm can survive for about seventy-two hours in the genital tract. So, in theory, if the couple abstain from sexual intercourse for three days each side of the *supposed* time of ovulation, pregnancy should not occur. Unfortunately, ovulation can occur at other times in the cycle, under the spur of emotion or stress or because the woman's cycle is irregular anyway. To overcome this, attempts are made to pinpoint ovulation by noting the rise of temperature which indicates onset and, more recently, by vaginal mucus tests. Even so, it is *not* a recommended method.

The second, and even more unreliable, method of contraception available to those who do not wish to have any artificial interference is coitus interruptus, or the 'withdrawal method', when the man withdraws his penis from the vagina just before ejaculation. But sperm ejaculated just outside the vagina can still make their way up to the uterus, and another risk is that the pre-ejaculatory fluid can contain some sperm.

Whichever method of contraception is used any instructions given by the doctor must be followed. If this is not done there is a high risk of pregnancy occurring.

It is not often that a woman becomes pregnant without knowing who is the father. If you are pregnant, or have fathered a pregnancy, then admit it as soon as possible.

Pregnancy scares are common among women in their teens and early twenties. They are due to the late onset of menstruation caused by irregular hormonal changes, which makes the woman think she is pregnant. It takes some time for the menstrual cycle to regularise itself and some women may well have left university before their periods happen every twenty-eight to thirty days. If menstruation is more than a week late then a woman may be pregnant. If your period is late and you suspect pregnancy then go to the health centre and ask for a pregnancy test. You will need to take a sample of urine passed first thing in the morning. The result will be back in a day or two. If the result is positive you will, along with your partner, have to decide exactly what to do. Whatever your decision, tell your parents, your department, and your doctor.

For expectant parents there are some further decisions to make. You must decide whether or not to remain single, or to get married. The baby could be fostered out until you finish your course, or even adopted. These are not easy decisions to make and all the possibilities will have to be discussed fully.

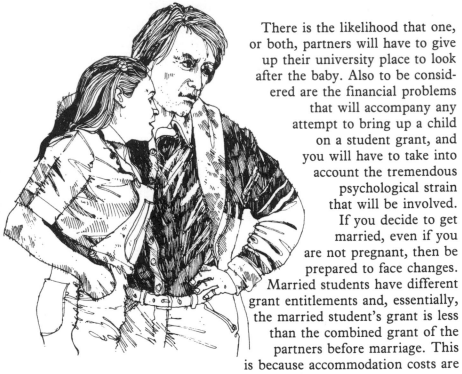

There is the likelihood that one, or both, partners will have to give up their university place to look after the baby. Also to be considered are the financial problems that will accompany any attempt to bring up a child on a student grant, and you will have to take into account the tremendous psychological strain that will be involved.

If you decide to get married, even if you are not pregnant, then be prepared to face changes. Married students have different grant entitlements and, essentially, the married student's grant is less than the combined grant of the partners before marriage. This is because accommodation costs are proportionally lower for married students.

Another problem for married students is finding suitable accommodation. Low priced flats are in short supply for young married couples, and it is unlikely that newly-weds will want to share a house or flat with other students. If you intend getting married, see the accommodation officer at the earliest opportunity. You must also be prepared to lose some of your independence and to have your studies interrupted more often. The need for a flexible timetable is vital.

Should you decide that you cannot face pregnancy and parenthood then an abortion may be the only alternative. This is a difficult decision to make and many people have strong objections arising from both moral and religious principles. An abortion is legal up to twenty-eight weeks, though this term is likely to be reduced. In any case the earlier a termination is sought and obtained the better as up to three months it involves only a simple operation. This usually requires one night in a hospital or clinic, though in some areas daytime abortions are performed in the early stages of pregnancy.

Under the 1967 Abortion Act the law requires examination by two doctors and their agreement that termination is justified. Your student health centre is the best starting point as a rule but availability of NHS abortions unfortunately varies very much from area to area. The British Pregnancy Advisory Service, a registered charity, helps to fill the gaps in areas like Birmingham and Wolverhampton where, in the past, NHS abortions have been difficult to obtain. BPAS abortions are not free but they are subsidized so that the cost is kept to a minimum and loans can sometimes be obtained. They are carried out in their own clinics, which are licensed and well run. There should be no need for any woman to seek the old and dangerous back street abortion, where mutilation, infertility and sometimes death could be the result.

Getting an *early* termination depends upon getting an *early* pregnancy test. Do-it-yourself testing kits are not fully reliable and should be considered only as a preliminary check. It is best to seek the advice of your own doctor or student health centre, but if for any reason you do not want to do this then a confidential pregnancy test can be arranged through your local Family Planning Clinic, Brook Clinic or BPAS. Citizens Advice Bureaux and local Welfare Officers may also be able to steer you in the right direction.

Abortion after four months of pregnancy and onwards involves more complex techniques and a longer stay in hospital. It is also relatively more risky and often far more emotionally disturbing, so seek help promptly.

Following advice about contraception should eliminate worries about pregnancy or abortion, but anyone who has sex with a number of different partners will have to face the possibility of suffering from a sexually transmitted disease. These diseases are becoming more and more common but, despite old wives' tales, they cannot be caught from lavatory seats, or dirty towels. Infection is passed on only through sexual contact, which does not necessarily mean intercourse.

Syphilis and gonorrhea are the most talked about sexually transmitted diseases and are unfortunately on the increase in the western world. After an active period they can lie dormant for years and constitute a serious threat to health and to children born to still infected women. It is vital to obtain treatment and to avoid spread, if infection is confirmed, contact should be made with other sexual partners involved. Although the diseases respond to modern antibiotics extremely well some thirteen per cent of women infected with gonorrhea lose their fertility, even after just one severe attack, if it involves the fallopian tubes. Symptoms include a burning sensation during urination and a discharge, but these can also be symptoms of far less serious and non-specific genital tract infections. Syphilis is characterised by a special type of ulcer on the genitals.

The most common sexually transmitted diseases are those caused by virus infection — over half a million new cases are treated in Britain every year — and they can sometimes be resistant to drugs. Symptoms may be similar to those of gonorrhea but some forms of infection in women do not produce any warning symptoms at all.

Other genital infections not necessarily sexually transmitted more often actively affect women but can be carried by men, so that it is best for both partners to be treated. One of the most common is monilia (thrush) also called candidiasis. This produces itching and burning and a white discharge caused by a yeast organism rather like fungus. Good treatments abound now for this condition which in the past so often made life a misery for girls. Anti-yeast creams, pessaries and tablets are all available on prescription and no girl should hesitate or feel shy about consulting a doctor or student health centre. Modern preparations enable these conditions to be cleared up in a few days. If a girl is having intercourse it is wise for the male partner to be prescribed a course of tablets to prevent reinfection.

Trichomonas is even more common perhaps than thrush, with ten per cent of women carrying the little organism which can cause inflammation, itching of the vulva and vagina and this time a greenish discharge. All these infections can remain dormant and then flare up but all, fortunately, can be treated.

Cystitis and other urinary tract infections, which again affect women more often than men, usually come from bacteria which normally live in the bowel. Transferred in any way to the bladder they can cause frequency and pain with cloudy urine and sometimes traces of blood. The first step is to take a specimen to your doctor. It is better still to provide a sterile mid-stream specimen at the surgery — full privacy is of course given and the results of the tests can be more accurate.

No woman today should suffer from either painful periods or from what used to be termed pre-menstrual tension and is now more often called pre-menstrual syndrome. The Pill can be helpful in controlling period pain and PMS can be treated successfully in nearly all cases by correcting the hormone levels now known to cause the problem.

Additional reading matter on such health problems and on sexual relationships is suggested in Further Advice on page 146.

Women seem to get more than their fair share of problems associated with sexual matters, not least of which is rape. Rape is forced sexual intercourse without permission, and is a criminal act. If you are assaulted then try not to panic. If you can manage to get a clear impression of your attacker it will help when describing him to the police. It is instinctive to struggle but this could increase the chances of serious injury. If you keep calm and offer no immediate threat to your attacker you may get an opportunity to escape. Rapists are usually sick in the mind and need careful handling to avoid provocation of a violent attack. Report the rape to the police as soon as possible. Ask them to withhold your name if you do not wish to be identified — all women find it distressing to admit that they have been raped. If you want sympathy and advice, contact some close friends or the Rape Crisis Centre, the address of which is listed in the Student Directory on page 140.

Hopefully, though, traumatic situations will never arise in your sexual life. Safe methods of contraception should prevent unwanted pregnancy and if you seek advice with any relationship difficulties you will be happy and able to study properly.

7 Politics

Most university students do not get involved with politics; generally, the popular image of an activist is certainly not true. Those students who do become involved in political activities usually join one of the many groups which are run by the student union. These groups include such clubs and societies as the Conservative Society and the International Socialists Society. There are other societies to represent different political and ideological views and many of them are organised on a national basis, with each university or college having a representative.

Political clubs and societies organise debates and discussions, and talks by leading politicians. They also promote their own political viewpoint and attempt to win supporters. In addition, their members have the opportunity to become actively involved in politics and many students carry on these activities after they graduate, perhaps even as far as the House of Commons.

As well as joining particular political groups some students become involved with the local student union, or the National Union of Students. Student unions at each college or university

York University buildings by the lake

represent students to the authorities. This is their main function and is achieved by having union representatives on most university committees. Some universities also have student representatives on the governing body, often called 'Senate'. The union representatives can put forward the views of students on the matters which are discussed by the various committees, a practice which is welcomed by most university authorities.

Most student unions are organised at three distinct levels. There are full time staff, an elected part time executive committee, and the general meeting.

The full time staff includes a small number of 'sabbatical' officers. These are students who have given up a year of studying in order to work for the union. The most common sabbatical posts are those of union president and vice-president, although there are others such as treasurer, or sports administrator, and so on. The sabbatical officers are the main representatives of the students to the university, and are also responsible for running the union. For this task they have the assistance of some full time staff which includes secretarial and administrative help, and accountants. The union might also employ a receptionist, a travel office administrator, and other ancillary staff, such as a bar manager or a catering manager.

The sabbatical officers will be part of the executive committee, or 'executive' as it is referred to. This committee consists of a number of elected students and is responsible for overseeing the day to day affairs of the union and for formulating its policy. The executive is usually elected at the general meeting.

General meetings are held a few times each term. They are open meetings at which all students can put their point of view, ask the executive to act on some matter, and elect representatives to university committees. Complaints can be voiced at these meetings if the executive is believed to be formulating poor policies, or is being unrepresentative.

It is worthwhile noting one exception to this form of union organisation. The University of Surrey Student Union is unique in that it does not have an executive. It is run by twice weekly general meetings, which are responsible for policy and the general day to day affairs of the union. The officers of this union claim that the lack of an executive at Surrey means the union is much more democratic and, consequently, more representative of the students as a whole.

Student representation usually attempts only to ensure fairness of treatment. It is rare to find student reps who voice political ideologies in committee meetings at the expense of student opinion and needs. Consequently, student unions deal with such matters as grants and finance, accommodation, welfare, education, and general university facilities. The student reps seek improvements in these areas if necessary and help the university in its development of these facilities.

The union has one other major task — it is responsible for the running of all the clubs and societies. Although each club is autonomous, the student union provides finance, facilities and advice.

In addition to these main tasks the student union provides a range of services to meet the needs of individual students. There will probably be a travel office in your union, and an Endsleigh insurance office. There will be legal and welfare advice, and help with finance if you are in difficulties. The student union will also take up individual cases of complaint against the university and will listen to any suggestions for improving the university or the union.

Student unions are financed by money raised by the university authorities. The amount each union receives depends on the number of students and the facilities the union provides. In addition, some unions raise small amounts of extra cash from bar takings and catering facilities.

Most unions will forward a small proportion of their income to the National Union of Students. If your union forwards money in this way you will automatically become a member of the NUS. However, not all student unions are affiliated to the NUS — indeed, Glasgow students union never has been — so check before you start using any NUS facilities that you are a member.

Like each individual college union, the NUS aims to represent the views of its members and to provide them with services and facilities. But the NUS is also politically active, a role which has grown out of the union's complicated history. The roots of the NUS can be traced back to Oxford University in the nineteenth century. The university's debating group became known as 'The United Debating Society'. This led to Manchester University students forming a 'Men's Union' in 1861.

It was universities in Scotland which led the way in student representation. At Edinburgh University in 1884 a Students' Representatives Council (SRC) was formed. It did not receive official recognition for five years, but this still preceded the formation of the first SRC in England. This was at Liverpool University in 1890.

The first English SRC to get official recognition was at Birmingham in 1900. Throughout the formative years in the late nineteenth and early twentieth centuries, universities actively disapproved of the SRCs and the unions. Before World War I, a national group of students was formed with the title of 'The British Student Congress'. This led to the formation of the National Union of Students in 1922. A Scottish Union of Students followed in the 1930s and this joined the NUS in 1971.

The NUS was founded in order to represent British students in an international group formed in Prague in 1921. This was called the 'Confédération Internationale des Étudiants'.

The original aim of the NUS as part of this international group was:

'To represent past and present students from a national and international point of view and to render possible the co-operation of the body of students in England, Wales, Scotland, and Ireland, with the students of other lands.'

Later the organisers of the NUS added another aim:

'To promote the educational and social interests of students in entire independence of all political or religious propaganda.'

To this end the NUS formed a travel service and a vacation work department, and by the 1930s it had established a loans system for students suffering severe financial hardship.

Gradually, the NUS found it increasingly difficult to achieve its second aim without bringing politics into its activities. The NUS adopted right wing policies and in 1926, the year of the General Strike, students were seen as strike breakers.

By the 1940s the union had become moderate and campaigned successfully for the introduction of mandatory grants and the need for all teachers to gain training certificates. The NUS was beginning its tradition of representing students and improving their status.

Gradually, the union moved back to the right wing of politics and its membership fell dramatically by twenty per cent. The union had largely become concerned with international affairs, meeting its original aim. The International Union of Students was formed, with the NUS president as its chairman. The seeming decrease in interest in home students provoked protests in the 1960s and eventually the NUS withdrew its support of the IUS.

This was closely followed by an attack on the right wing policies of the NUS. The Radical Students Alliance and a rival group, the Revolutionary Socialist Students Federation, were set up in the mid 1960s. The union gradually moderated and by the 1970s had moved to the left wing of politics. In the 1980s the NUS is dominated by left wing politicians, although the Federation of Conservative Students remains the largest student political organisation in the United Kingdom.

Although the NUS is dominated by left wing leaders, its main aims are not political. Like individual student unions the NUS strives to represent its members to the authorities. It submits information and requests to such bodies as the Department of

The Chapel at Pembroke College, Cambridge was Sir Christopher Wren's first architectural venture

(*above*) The High Street, Exeter. The Guildhall, on the left, is the oldest municipal building in Britain; (*below*) Edinburgh Castle, dating largely from the sixteenth century, occupies a commanding site overlooking the city

The nave of Bristol Cathedral. Founded as an Augustinian monastery in 1140, the cathedral has been developed continuously for the past 800 years

The Register House, Edinburgh, was built between 1774 and 1789 from designs by Robert Adam. It houses the Scottish Record Office

Education and Science, the Committee of Vice-Chancellors and Principals, or the Universities Grants Committee.

In addition to representing students on a national basis, the NUS will help individual unions, or individual students, with particular problems, or campaigns. The NUS has a staff of more than seventy people who are experts in handling such problems as claiming supplementary benefits, or dealing with unhelpful university authorities, and so on.

The NUS also runs the National Student Discount Scheme, NUS Marketing, and Great Stuff Records. It lends its support to Endsleigh Insurance Services, helps with providing cheap student travel and holidays, and deals with vacation work and careers generally.

National Student is a free monthly newspaper produced by the NUS for all its members, and it is valuable for keeping students up to date with the news of universities and colleges. *National Student* also carries a variety of background features on such topics as careers and travel.

The NUS is not politically inactive, though. It does take a particular stance on some important issues at home and abroad, lobbying parliament and contributing to any associated protests if necessary. Which issues should be taken up, and how they should be approached, are decided by 'conference'. This is the governing body of the NUS, which lays down its policy, elects the executive, and dictates how the Union should be run.

This annual conference is a meeting of representatives of all the NUS affiliated universities and colleges in the United Kingdom. These representatives will have been told by their own unions what to vote for and how they should vote. These decisions are made in general meetings up and down the country, and the representatives are chosen either by the general meetings or, in large colleges, by a ballot of all the students.

Conference elects the National Executive Committee (NEC) which is responsible for the day to day running of the NUS affairs. About a third of the members of the NEC work full time at the NUS headquarters in London. The rest are part timers and often have special responsibilities for particular areas.

The NUS, like local unions, also has a number of full time staff such as accountants, secretaries, administrators, researchers, and public relations officers. All of these people work under the instructions of the NEC. As the NEC operates under the instructions of conference, which is representative of all students, the NUS is really run by the student body as a whole.

If you feel that the NUS is not representing your viewpoint, or that the NEC is not performing its duties as it should, then the situation can be changed. The procedure is to go through your representatives to conference. These people must vote according to the instructions of their union general meeting. If you want to change matters, present a motion to your general meeting and attempt to get it approved. If other students agree with you, then your delegate to conference must vote accordingly. However, you might be alone in your views and the delegate would have to vote as instructed. The NUS, and its associated local unions, pride themselves on a high level of democracy. This democracy cannot work properly unless individual students become involved in the decision making. If you are upset by what your union is doing, or by the NUS, then matters can only be altered by your going to the general meeting and getting a motion approved.

Presenting motions to general meetings is a process which varies between different unions but, basically, the principles are the same. A formal written motion must be submitted to the chairman some time before the meeting, and the proposal must be seconded. In other words, it must carry the signature of one other person who agrees with the motion.

The motion will then be included on the agenda for the meeting and the proposer will be invited to make a speech on the matter. Naturally, there will probably be an opposing speech, as in debates. There will be some discussion, then a vote will be taken and the motion will be lost or carried. It is often a good idea to drum up support for a motion from fellow students as this will help swell the numbers of people who will vote in favour. This is an established method of winning in debates of this nature.

You might find that you enjoy taking part in the general meetings and will want to become involved with the running of the union. If this is so, then talk about this to the executive and ask the members how to go about joining them, or working for the NUS. If you have definite political leanings then join the relevant society and get involved in its running. Local political groups might also be looking for support from students.

While at university you will probably become involved in student politics infrequently, unless you are particularly interested. However, it is likely that you will get involved with national or local political elections.

Once you reach the age of eighteen your name will be registered on a list of electors, people eligible to vote in elections. You will almost certainly be registered at your parents' address, but the university will also register you. This does not mean that when an election is due you will get the chance to vote twice, as it is illegal to vote more than once in any British election. You must decide where you want to vote — in your home town, or in the university town. Instructions about voting will automatically be sent in both areas. However, if your home town is some distance away from the university, you will be entitled to apply to the 'Returning Officer' for a postal vote should you wish to vote at home. In this case the vote in your university town becomes invalid.

For many students voting in elections is their only political activity. But your union, and the NUS, depend on individual students to make them work. If you deny support to your union you may well be denying youself better facilities or services.

Durham

8 Holidays and Travel

As a student you will spend almost half of each year on holiday. University vacations last for about twenty-two weeks a year, longer for some colleges. This means that you will need to find something to do to prevent boredom. The range of possible activities is enormous but most students take up some form of part time employment. Short term jobs are available mainly during the summer vacation, although there is a restricted number of jobs to be found during the Christmas and Easter breaks.

The reasons for doing vacation work vary but, generally, most students need the money. Student grants do not always provide enough cash to complete the term without going into a bank overdraft. In order to see them through the expenses of the vacation and to repay the overdraft many students just have to get a job. Other students work to save up some money for a special item, or because they cannot face the long holiday without some occupation.

Getting a holiday job is not easy. There is intense competition for vacation employment and every year thousands of students are disappointed. In times of economic depression and high unemployment the number of student holiday jobs can be dramatically reduced. Disappointment can be avoided by applying early for the sort of jobs you want. For employment during the Christmas vacation you should apply in the summer, and for jobs during the long break it is advisable to apply during the early part of the spring term. If your application is too early the employer will tell you when to re-apply.

When applying for work, point out that you are only seeking a temporary placement. Your application should be polite, neat and tidy and contain all the relevant details. What details to include and how to write an application is dealt with in chapter 9.

The most popular Christmas vacation job is delivering post. The Post Office employs a large number of temporary postmen and postwomen during the few weeks leading up to Christmas in order to clear the enormous mountain of mail. If you want to work as a Christmas postman then apply to the Head Postmaster of your nearest main Post Office, just before the start of the autumn term. The competition will be intense, so apply for some other jobs as well.

Another line of work for students at Christmas is restaurant or hotel employment. Many of these establishments are on the look out for waiters or bar staff, but remember that you might be expected to work on Christmas Day. Pubs and clubs are also grateful for extra bar staff in the couple of weeks around Christmas and New Year festivities.

Working in a bar can be done in all holidays. In the summer vacation bar staff are in demand at holiday resorts, where there are also jobs for deck chair attendants, ice cream salesmen, bus conductors, hotel workers, and bingo callers to name just a few.

There is an annual publication, *Summer Jobs in Britain*, which is sold in university bookshops and it lists all the employers who are looking for short term staff. Also consult the Vacation Work Bulletin published by the National Union of Students.

Many students get summer jobs at holiday camps, working as bar staff, waiters, childminders, secretaries, cleaners, entertainers, disc-jockeys, bus drivers, fun-fair operators, and so on. Such vacancies are often notified to careers offices, and the staff will be glad to help you with applications. Other occupations, especially during the Easter vacation, include factory work, farming, labouring, secretarial temping and shop work. Unusual student jobs can be found as a town guide, a nursery school assistant, or even as a zoo keeper. These varied jobs are usually available only to students with specialist experience, or who are following relevant courses.

Working abroad is possible, especially during the summer. Most of the jobs are in Europe and America and are listed in the guide *Summer Jobs Abroad*. There are jobs at holiday resorts and camps, just as in the UK, and language students might be able to get work as guides or couriers. Fruit picking and working in vineyards is popular in Europe. Occasionally women students can get some au-pair work.

In America you can work in one of the summer camps

organised for children and teenagers. The camp jobs are varied — you could be a swimming instructor or perhaps a stamp collecting tutor. The pay is not very high but you do get an opportunity to visit the USA, and food and board are free. BUNACAMP, the British Universities North America Camp, and Camp America are the two organisations to contact. Your university might have a representative of one or both of these groups but, if not, the addresses are listed in the Student Directory.

If you do manage to get a holiday job you might earn enough money to become liable for income tax. The amount is calculated on the earnings received for a year. Although you will probably be working for only three or four months each year, your holiday earnings will be taxed unless you ask the local tax office for exemption, explaining that you are a student. The officer will send your employer a form for you both to complete. The tax office can then authorise the payment of your wages without any tax deductions. If you do not get this authorisation before starting work, any tax paid can be refunded on application to the tax office, but it may take many weeks. Similarly, if you are employed during a 'sandwich' course you can claim tax refunds on any earnings below the level of taxable income.

There are some state benefits which students can claim during vacations, if they cannot find work. Supplementary benefit is a means tested award and so there is no standard amount of money paid to all students. The money is available only to those who can prove that the vacation element of their grant does not cover their expenses. Usually help is needed to pay rent as the vacation element does not include money for this. The supplementary benefit received is, therefore, going to be roughly equivalent to the rent. However, the vacation element only applies to the Christmas and Easter vacations, so a student eligible for the benefit during the summer is likely to get a larger sum than during the short breaks. When applying for supplementary benefit it is worthwhile noting that the Department of Health and Social Security, which administers the award and makes assessments, assumes that all students get a full grant, regardless of parental contributions.

The process of claiming supplementary benefit is complicated and a whole day should be set aside in order to deal with the formalities. First, you have to register for work at the nearest

Jobcentre. If there are no jobs available, then register as unemployed at the unemployment benefit office. However, you will not be allowed to claim unemployment benefit unless you have worked before and paid a sufficient amount of money into the National Insurance scheme. If this is not the case, then claim supplementary benefit by registering with the social security office after you have registered as unemployed.

At the social security office explain that you are a student seeking supplementary benefit. You will be asked to complete a form and attend an interview. When you go for this interview, which may be some days later, take some form of identification — a birth certificate or a NHS medical card will do. Also take some proof of the amount of rent you will be paying during the vacation and some evidence of the dates of the holiday. Benefit will be sent in the form of a Girocheque, which can be cashed at a Post Office or paid into your bank account. You might be expected to sign for this money each week at the social security office and failure to do so could mean losing benefit.

You will not be eligible for supplementary benefit if you are not paying any rent at Christmas or Easter because your vacation element is supposed to cover all other expenses. In the summer you will be entitled to receive some money, usually the same as the vacation element, which is not included in the summer term grant. Also, supplementary benefit will not be paid if you are working or are eligible for unemployment benefit.

If you do have some cash available you might want to go away on holiday. Choosing the right holiday at the right price can be a tricky business. Most universities have a student travel office where the staff are very helpful and can give advice about specific holiday requirements. If your college has no such service then go to a travel agent who specialises in arranging holidays for students. The largest of these specialist agencies is 'London Student Travel', which is listed in the Student Directory.

If you go to any other travel agent, make sure that the agency is registered with the Association of British Travel Agents (ABTA). This can be checked quite easily as all ABTA members display their membership sign in their windows. ABTA provides greater protection against your holiday going wrong and a standard complaints procedure if the holiday was spoilt or cost more than you were originally told.

Package holidays are organised by tour operators and provide all needs, such as hotel and transport, in a single transaction. If you want to go independently, all the different aspects of your holiday will have to be booked separately. The advantage of 'go it alone' holidays is that you are not tied to the arrangements made by tour operators, but the disadvantage is that they can be more expensive than package deals, although cheaper air fares and special student rates are changing this.

Brochures are produced by all the tour operators to help you choose a holiday. But, remember, these brochures are nothing more than advertisements and can sometimes be, unintentionally, misleading. Read them carefully and ask the travel agent specific questions about the holidays. The agent will be receiving ten per cent of what you pay, so he should be expected to work for the money.

Before booking a holiday, check how much it is going to cost and exactly what you will get for the money. Ask if there are any extras to be paid for and whether or not insurance is provided. Find out what protection you have if the hotel is overbooked or something else goes wrong. Do not pay the travel agent any money until you are satisfied with the holiday you are being offered and the price you are expected to pay.

Having decided on a holiday, you will be expected to pay a deposit of about ten per cent of the total cost. On paying this, ask for written confirmation of your booking together with the agreed terms and conditions of the holiday. This written statement will help if there is cause to complain later. The total payment is usually due two months before the holiday starts.

Check the details of what you will need to pack. If you have booked a self-catering holiday you might need to take sheets, for example. If you are going abroad you will need an up to date passport. If you have not got a passport, apply for one as soon as possible. It can take two months to process the information so, if you are going abroad in the summer, apply for your passport early in the spring.

Application forms for full British passports are available in main Post Offices. The form will have to be signed by a responsible person who is not a member of your family — your personal tutor, bank manager, or doctor will do this. You will also need two small photographs of yourself, one of which must also be signed by a responsible person. Submit the form to the address for your area and enclose the fee, together with your birth certificate as proof of identity.

If you are travelling to western Europe or Canada you can use a British visitors' passport. This is much cheaper than a full passport but it lasts for only one year. There is no need for the signature of a responsible person and a visitors' passport can be bought across the counter at main Post Offices.

In addition to a passport, some countries, such as the USA, require an entry visa before visitors can be admitted. If your holiday has been arranged through a travel agent then your visas will probably have been obtained, but check with the agency. If you are arranging your own holiday, obtain your visas at the earliest opportunity from the embassies of the relevant countries. You might also need some vaccinations against diseases which are prevalent in other countries. Go to your doctor for advice, and be prepared to pay a small fee for any injections.

If you are travelling abroad you will need the right currency for the particular country you will be visiting, or arrangements to obtain cash on arrival. Foreign currency can be bought from most British banks. Travellers cheques can also be bought from your bank and these are safer than currency, which can be lost. If travellers cheques are lost your bank will normally be able to make arrangements for their replacement. You can also get money abroad with some credit cards and the Eurocheque card will guarantee sterling cheques in Europe.

If you find that something has gone wrong with your holiday, make a complaint to the hotel manager, the holiday camp organiser, or someone in charge. If you are on a package holiday speak to the local representative of the tour operator or get in touch with the travel agent.

If you are abroad and find yourself in trouble with the police, or you are stranded without money, or find that everything has gone completely wrong, then contact the British consul. He will be at one of the British Consulates situated in the biggest cities of the country you are in.

If your holiday has not lived up to expectations, or was not as described in the brochure, take your case in the first instance to the travel agent. If he takes no action, or gives an unsatisfactory reply, take your complaint to ABTA, who can help to negotiate compensation. But don't forget that they cannot help unless the travel agent is a member. If you still have cause to complain after speaking to ABTA take your case to the Office of Fair Trading.

If you want to arrange your own holiday abroad, take advantage of the cheap travel arrangements available to students. There are a number of different ways of obtaining cheap air travel and the best method will depend upon your destination. Check out the cheapest with your nearest student travel office or with London Student Travel.

You can also get cheap rail fares for Europe through Transalpino, a company which offers special reductions to students. Many students take advantage of these offers and tour Europe for a few weeks during the summer. They can travel to and from most destinations, according to their own route, and can travel at times of their own choice. If you are travelling in the UK or to the Channel Islands, or Ireland, take advantage of the Student Rail Card, which can get you many tickets at half price.

If you are booking accommodation, make sure that the hotel or inn has a good reputation and provides clean, comfortable rooms. In England, Wales and Scotland the various tourist boards publish guides for visitors and these include lists of suitable accommodation. The tourist departments of European countries can help you find good accommodation and travel agents are helpful, although you will have to pay for their service.

Camping can be exciting and challenging but, without preparation, this type of holiday could become a disaster. The rule to remember is to have enough of the right sort of equipment. A tent without a groundsheet will be useless if it is raining, and a cylinder of gas is no good without the stove to go with it. When you go camping, make sure that you use official camping sites, especially if travelling abroad. If you camp anywhere you like there could be trouble with landowners, and if you do get permission to camp on private land you could find yourself robbed or attacked. For your own safety, use an official site where there are many other campers. The Camping Club will be able to tell you where to go and you can join the club for a small fee if you are going camping regularly.

Youth hostelling is a favourite form of holiday for students, especially for those interested in rambling or other outdoor pursuits. The hostels, found throughout the world, provide accommodation for members of the Youth Hostels Association. You can join by applying to the head office, listed in the Student Directory.

If you want to go on a hitch hiking holiday, where you book accommodation in advance, or take a tent, and rely on others for transport, you should be aware of the risks involved. Some students hitch hike, or 'thumb-it', between home and university. In either case you can spend a long time trying to arrange a lift without getting very far. When you do get a lift there is some chance of being robbed or attacked. Women, especially, should be aware of the dangers of hitching, particularly if they take up this type of holiday alone. If you are hitch hiking abroad, check that there are no laws against it.

Whatever form of holiday you choose do not take any risks. Make sure that you have access to enough money to see you through any problems. Always carry some form of identification — this should be your passport if you are travelling abroad. Make sure that you are insured, especially for your health abroad. Other countries do not have the elaborate NHS organisation available in the UK and, if you fall ill abroad, you could face large medical bills.

Travelling and holidays will probably be restricted to the summer vacation. During the shorter vacations there may not be enough time to go away. That may sound surprising, but academic work is not confined to term time.

You will be expected to continue studying throughout the year, including all three vacations. There will probably be some work to complete, such as essays, before the beginning of the next term. During the Easter break you will probably be revising for examinations, which often occur during the first few weeks of the summer term.

As you did during term time, draw up a personal timetable (see page 33). This should include family commitments, your holiday, vacation work, social occasions, as well as your study. Do not get lazy during the holiday and stay in bed all morning just because there are no lectures to attend but, equally, do not spent all of the vacation studying. Relax and take some time off. The studying done during holidays should be a review of the previous term's work. Be sure that you understand any aspects of the course which you found difficult. Vacations are also useful for reading general books about your subject and for learning more about particular topics which interest you.

If you give up studying altogether during the vacations it will be difficult to get back into the swing of things at the beginning of the next term. You will have forgotten some things and find it hard to understand some lectures, which means that your studies will deteriorate rapidly.

Before returning to university, check that you have completed all the set work. Also check the date on which term starts and arrange to arrive on the afternoon before. This will give you time to settle in and have a friendly social evening with people you have not seen for some while, then you will be ready to forget your holiday and begin a new term of studying.

9 Careers and Postgraduate Studies

It is never too early to consider what you want to do when you graduate. In fact, the earlier you do start thinking about the future the better. Those students who postpone making any decisions until the last few weeks of their final year may be losing the chance of a good job and a promising career.

Most first year students fall into two categories as far as career decisions are concerned — they either have a definite idea as to the type of job they want, or no idea whatsoever. You may feel pretty sure about the career you want but don't be surprised if later in your course you change your mind. This happens to thousands of students.

However, if you do not know what career to follow then there is no better place for advice than your careers office. These are run by expert careers advisers who know how to fit students' hopes and aspirations into particular lines of employment. They know where the job vacancies are and they can help arrange interviews. The careers advisers are usually helped by a number of ancillary staff who run a library and a general information service. Most careers office libraries are well stocked with

The Senate House, Cambridge

leaflets, books and pamphlets about a whole range of careers and on organisations which offer employment to graduates. Take advantage of this library and make regular visits while choosing a career.

The careers office staff will also be prepared to discuss any aspect of university life. You might feel that your chosen course is not suitable and that a change is necessary. The careers adviser will discuss the opportunities for change and point out the options open. Most universities will allow students to change courses during their first year, but not after that.

Choosing a career is not easy. There are a number of things to be taken into consideration, not least of which is job compatibility. Occupational psychologists have devised a number of tests for determining which type of people fit best into certain occupations. Your careers adviser should have access to 'aptitude tests' if you want to take one. Some commercial companies also offer these tests, and the services of an occupational psychologist, but their charges will be high. Other factors which will influence your decision include anticipated level of earnings, geographical preference, the responsibilities you are prepared to take, and the general style of life you would like to have.

Sometimes the degree course you are following may decide your career; for example, you might be studying medicine or chemical engineering. The majority of students on such highly vocational courses continue on to jobs in the relevant professions. Most medical students become general practitioners or hospital doctors, but some become administrators in the National Health Service or work for a pharmaceutical company. Similarly, other vocationally orientated courses do not necessarily limit your choice of a job.

Most employers of graduates start looking for staff at the beginning of the spring term and their advertising is directed at final year students. But many companies expect applications well before this time of year and so students approaching graduation really should come to a decision during the winter term.

Vacant positions are advertised in the national and local press or, alternatively, you could apply to any of the companies which take part in the annual scheme organised by the careers service. This involves companies and organisations visiting universities and polytechnics to interview prospective employees.

Another method of obtaining employment is to write a letter to any company for which you would like to work asking if there are any vacancies. Often such letters will produce no immediate results but your name may be kept on file and you could be contacted in the future.

At some stage during your search for a job you will probably be expected to complete an application form. These forms vary from simple affairs to lengthy and complicated booklets. Read them carefully and make sure that your application is presentable. The best method is to assemble all the information you need before filling in the form. Since you will probably be completing more than one application it may be useful to compile a series of notes in a small document file. These notes should include all the basic background information about yourself such as address, date of birth, schools attended, educational qualifications, and details of previous employment or any specialist experience. They should also include some brief details about your interests and hobbies and the names and addresses of two people who are prepared to act as referees.

It is best to complete forms in black ink as some companies will make copies of your application. Write in block capitals for legibility, and do not cram your answers. A well laid out form will create a good impression with any prospective employer. Remember that your application form will be used as the basis for any future interviews, so be totally honest and try to avoid ambiguities. Make a copy of the application before posting. Enclosing a stamped, self addressed envelope may help to bring a prompt reply.

On many occasions you will need to apply for a position in the form of a letter, and its presentation will be an advertisement for yourself. In writing letters to employers, follow the same basic principles as for completing application forms. Gather all the information needed, be legible and create an attractive layout.

The first paragraph should mention the job you are applying for and the reasons for your interest. In the next paragraph write briefly about yourself and draw attention to any facts which demonstrate your suitability for the job. Do not include too much information but refer to your curriculum vitae, an example of which is shown on page 118. Such a CV should not take up more than one side of A4 paper — the employer does not want to have to wade through reams of details.

Curriculum Vitae

Name: Brian Smith   Age: 21   Sex: Male

Marital status: Single   Nationality: British

Term time address: St Stephens Hall, Mudtown College, Mudtown

Home address: 13, The Cuttings, Edgbaston, Birmingham

Education

Edgbaston Primary School   1965 - 1971

Birmingham City Grammar School   1971 - 1978

Mudtown College   1978 - present

Qualifications

GCE O Levels   Eng. Language, Eng. Literature, Mathematics,

        History, French, Latin

GCE A Levels   Eng. Literature, French, Economics

Currently reading for BA(Hons) Eng. Literature graduating in June

Employment

Shelf filler   Tesco supermarket, Edgbaston, summer 1978

General assistant   Smith's Advertising, Mudtown, summer 1979 and 1980

Experience

School: Prefect, librarian, editor of sixth form newspaper

College: Member of debating society, cricket club captain,

        advertisement manager of student newspaper

Hobbies

Popular music, cricket, writing

Referees

Mr Ian Jones, 12, High Street, Edgbaston, Birmingham

Dr John Smith, Dept of English, Mudtown College, Mudtown

AN EXAMPLE OF A CURRICULUM VITAE

Brian Smith

St Stephens Hall

Mudtown College

Mudtown

The Personnel Officer

Magnificent Advertising

Slush Street

Mudtown   15 January

Dear Sir

I am a final year undergraduate of English Literature at Mudtown
College and I wish to pursue a career in advertising. I would like
to be considered for any vacancies for graduate trainees which you
might have this summer.

As shown on the enclosed curriculum vitae, I have gained some first
hand knowledge of the advertising industry by working for Smith's
Advertising as a general assistant during two summer vacations.

At university I have been involved in the running of the student newspaper, with special responsibility for the advertisements. I am keen
to become involved in advertising when I graduate in June this
year.

I hope my qualifications and experience will make me suitable for
consideration. I look forward to hearing from you.

Yours faithfully

Brian Smith

AN EXAMPLE OF AN APPLICATION LETTER

Sign off your letter with 'Yours faithfully', if you do not know the name of the person to whom you are writing, or 'Yours sincerely' if you do know. An example of a letter of application is shown on page 119.

Once you have applied for a job, it will probably be a few weeks before you hear anything. If the company does not reply within about one month, telephone them and ask if your letter has been received. If it has not, then check the address and send another copy.

Most job interviews for graduates take place during the spring term. They are generally initial interviews for a group of likely candidates, from which employers usually select a shortlist. The second interviews take place in the last part of the spring term and the beginning of the summer term. They are much more searching and are sometimes supplemented by tests.

Be prepared for interviews. You are, after all, being assessed, and if you create a good impression your chances of success will be higher. Do your homework on the company. Read all the available literature so that you can talk in an informed manner and ask relevant questions; having nothing to say will put you at a disadvantage. Arrive in good time for your interview and try to relax. During the interview try to establish a personal contact with the interviewer. Always give full answers to any questions. Simple 'yes' and 'no' answers will not give the interviewer a very clear picture of your personality.

If you are invited to attend a second interview, be prepared to answer questions of a very searching nature. You may also have to answer questions of an academic nature and be expected to take part in some form of test. This may be a standard IQ test or a specific aptitude test for the job. Whatever form it takes, treat the test like an exam. Read the instructions carefully, answer the questions as set, use your time appropriately for the number of questions, and present coherent answers.

The company may hold a panel interview, where candidates have to face more than one interviewer. Treat this style of interview as a normal interview. Make sure that you always look at the person who is asking the questions and direct your answer back to him. Once you have given your answer, turn your attention to the chairman of the panel to indicate that you are ready for another question.

Many second interviews are held over a couple of days, and

usually include tours of the company premises, meetings with recently appointed graduates, and so on. There could be some form of function, usually social, on the evening before your interview. The employers will pay all your expenses for attending these events.

After the second interview there will be some time to wait before anything is heard from the company. This time interval is extremely variable and if you have not heard within about ten days, write a polite letter asking when you are likely to be given a decision. If a job is offered, you might need a few days to consider it but it is wise to make a decision as soon as possible. If you do not want the job then turn down the offer, by letter, immediately. A delay in rejecting job offers could mean that other final years are denied the opportunity of employment.

If you have accepted a job and a better offer turns up before you graduate, an explanatory letter should be written to the company whose offer you first accepted. As a general rule this course of action should be avoided as it may prejudice your chances with the company in the future. If their time has been wasted once, they may not wish to take the risk again.

If no job offers are forthcoming during the spring term, seek some help from the careers advisers. They will have information about areas where there are vacancies, and they can help if you want to change your mind about the type of career to follow. You may need some more qualifications. These range from specialist diplomas and certificates, such as those for teaching or nursing, to higher degrees. If you do opt for any form of extra qualification you will have to take on postgraduate studies.

Postgraduates can be found at all universities and polytechnics, and at many colleges. All of them will tell you that the postgraduate student life is very different from their undergraduate days. There are usually no strict terms and most postgraduates work for about forty-five weeks of the year. For many types of postgraduates there are no grants available from local education authorities, so finances can often be a problem. The work is much more demanding and intense than undergraduate studies. If you cannot face these and other problems, do not consider becoming a postgraduate student.

The number of postgraduate courses available grows each year and, in addition, there are a large number of postgraduate students performing original research which does not follow any formal study pattern. If you want to gain a professional qualification, such as the postgraduate certificate of education (PGCE), then you will be following a formal course of lectures for about one full year. You could, however, opt for a Masters degree in a particular branch of your undergraduate work. These usually take one full year, although many universities do offer higher degrees on a part time basis.

Many postgraduates at universities and polytechnics are enrolled as research students aiming at doctorate qualifications. The most common of these is the Doctor of Philosophy and is awarded by most universities, and by the Council for National Academic Awards, for valuable research in any subject. The doctorate postgraduate courses last for a minimum of three years.

For students aiming at professional qualifications, grants are available from the professions and industry and, in some instances, from local education authorities. But research students do not qualify for these grants.

For these students, finance can be a problem. Indeed, some of them have to delay their postgraduate studies because they cannot obtain suitable financial support. If you want to become a research student, then finances should be arranged as soon as possible during your final undergraduate year. Most postgraduate research studies are financed by government sponsored research councils. These include the Science Research Council, the Social Sciences Research Council, the Agricultural Research Council, and the Arts Council. However, some students will be financed by sponsorship for industrial companies. The careers office and your department will be able to help you, as will the head of the relevant university department where you intend studying as a postgraduate.

Before finally deciding to become a postgraduate research student, discuss with your lecturers your aptitude for such work. You will only be accepted for doctor studies if you have achieved First or Upper Second Class Honours at an undergraduate level. If you and your lecturers do not think that you can achieve such high results, then do not opt for research studies.

Places for research students are notified to the careers service and, on occasions, advertised in journals. However, universities and polytechnics publish prospectuses for postgraduate students and these will list the areas of research and tell you how to apply. The prospectus will also include details about Masters degree courses and professional qualifications. University libraries usually have all the postgraduate prospectuses in the reference section. If you cannot find the one you want, send a short letter to the Registry of the relevant university requesting details of postgraduate studies.

If postgraduate studies are not feasible, or you have been unsuccessful in finding a job, you will, unfortunately, have to face the daunting prospect of unemployment. The first and most important thing to do after leaving university without a job is to register at the local Jobcentre. They might have some suitable employment and, if so, they will give you the details and help you arrange an interview. If no suitable work is available, register with the unemployment benefit office. This office will need to know your National Insurance number and details of any money earned in the previous year. When your registration has been approved you will be entitled to benefit each week until you get a job. If the unemployment benefit office cannot help, then go to the social security office. This office will award supplementary benefit if you have not paid enough money into the National Insurance scheme to receive unemployment benefit. As most students will not have paid any NI contributions they usually receive supplementary benefit if they are unemployed on graduation. Apply for this benefit as you did during your vacations (see page 107). Of course, do not give up applying for jobs. Write some 'on spec' letters and seek the help of your university careers advisers or local authority careers office.

Hopefully, you will be employed at the end of your university career, although you should face the reality of unemployment and the fact that it takes a significant number of graduates some time to find a satisfying job. When you start working there will be many new problems and there are a few basic facts with which you should be familiar.

Your employer should provide a written statement which outlines the terms and conditions of the job. Most employers will give you this contract before you start work but there is no legal requirement for them to do so at this time. They do have to provide this statement within thirteen weeks of the date you started working at the company. In addition, you should also receive a statement of earnings, and any deductions, every time you receive your salary.

The money earned will be taxed under the Pay As You Earn (PAYE) scheme. The employer deducts the relevant amount and forwards it to the tax office. You will also have to pay National Insurance contributions each week. If your employer makes an error in his deductions then point it out immediately.

It might be easier to make any complaints through a trade union. Unions represent their members on an individual or group basis to the employers, and also negotiate pay increases and changes in conditions for employees.

If you are a woman, you might feel discriminated against at work. Take any complaints about unfair treatment because of your sex to the Equal Opportunities Commission. Naturally, because of the history and tradition of male dominance in work, women often have more reason to suspect discrimination, but the commission will act on behalf of men as well.

Some students delay their employment and perform voluntary work for a year or so after leaving university. Organisations such as Voluntary Services Overseas (VSO) and Oxfam accept help

The Pfeiffer Building of Newnham College, Cambridge. Newnham, a
college for women, was founded in 1871

The pillared and domed building housing the National Museum of Wales, in Cardiff, was completed in 1927. It contains various interesting collections and has a gallery devoted to Welsh Folk Life

from graduates who want to work in underprivileged communities. The careers service will let you know if any places are available.

The careers staff will also see you after you have graduated and left the university. If you have any problems whatsoever with employment then their expert knowledge will prove invaluable.

10 The Open University

The largest university in the United Kingdom, the Open University, is unique. Its students study at home and those taking degree courses do not have to meet entrance requirements. Students of the OU are of all ages from twenty-one to seventy and have academic backgrounds ranging from people who left school at fourteen without taking examinations to highly qualified professors. Because of this, and because the Open University employs unusual study methods, the problems of those students will be quite different from those encountered at other universities.

The OU was established in 1969 as a result of an idea put forward by Harold Wilson some six years earlier when he was leader of the Labour party then in opposition. He announced his plans for the 'University of the Air', which would employ existing television and radio services as a means of teaching. The concept was not new. Adult education using radio and television was carried out successfully in the United States and the Soviet Union before the OU was considered seriously in the United Kingdom, although the BBC announced its hopes of a 'Broadcasting University' in June 1924.

It is this historical background to the Open University, and the BBC's long standing commitment to education, that gives rise to the belief that OU students spend many hours watching television or listening to the radio. In fact, broadcasting accounts for only ten per cent of their study

Peterhouse College, Cambridge

time, and some students do not listen to the OU programmes at all. The Open University teaches mainly with correspondence courses. In addition, it has a number of regional centres where tuition is given by part time lecturers.

The main degrees awarded by the Open University are BA and BA(Hons). The university also awards postgraduate degrees to research students and there are a number of short non-degree courses for associate students. The BA degrees are built up using a system of credits, an idea borrowed from American universities. At the OU, six credits are needed for the ordinary degree and eight credits for the honours degree. To gain each credit, students have to complete successfully a thirty-two week course which runs from late January to November. Each week is a single study unit and requires between ten and fourteen hours of work. This is roughly one third of the time spent studying by other university students, but OU students are getting degrees on a part time basis and this is why it can take eight years to get an honours degree.

All students are given a foundation course, which is a broad based introduction to their subject. After completing this, they can choose, from a varied range of courses, the aspects of their subject which they would most like to study. Consequently, every student of the OU has an individually tailored degree course.

For each course of thirty-two study units there are a number of set books. Students are expected to read these in conjunction with thirty-two study texts which are sent at regular intervals throughout the course. These texts are the basis of the OU teaching and include self-assessment questions for students to chart their own progress and to find out what they do not understand. The texts are supplemented by television and radio programmes produced by the OU in partnership with the BBC.

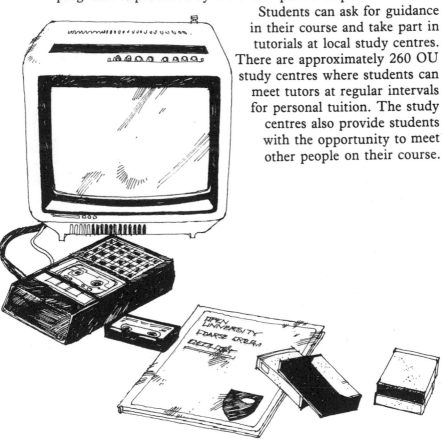

Students can ask for guidance in their course and take part in tutorials at local study centres. There are approximately 260 OU study centres where students can meet tutors at regular intervals for personal tuition. The study centres also provide students with the opportunity to meet other people on their course.

There is very little formal teaching at the OU. However, lectures, seminars and practical classes occurr at the compulsory Summer School. All students on foundation courses attend this school, which lasts for one week and is held at a campus university. Science students attend more than one Summer School and many courses have additional study weekends with formal teaching.

Credits are awarded by a process of continuous assessment, together with an examination held at the end of the thirty-two week course. The assessment is based on a number of assignments issued as part of the study units. Some assignments are marked by the tutors and some multiple choice tests are marked by computer. Science students are loaned 'Home Experiment Kits' and some of their assignments include practical work.

The study courses are units of programmed learning. This means that students have to complete each assignment by a certain date. There is no time allowed for OU students to give up on something they do not understand and repeat the work later. They must work to deadlines.

Unlike students of residential universities, OU students are alone. They do not have fellow students around all the time to help with, or check, their studies. Nor do they have easy access to well stocked libraries, laboratory facilities and instant expert tuition, all of which are available to resident students.

The problems of being a lone student are met every day by OU undergraduates, but the university has made tremendous efforts to overcome most difficulties. The OU has produced all of its own basic texts which are available to students and there is a growing collection of general OU books to be found in many bookshops. Tuition at study centres is arranged regularly and tutors are always available by telephone in emergencies.

If you are an OU student it is vital to keep in regular contact with your tutor. You will need advice and encouragement throughout your degree course and if the tutor does not get to know you, and understand your particular strengths and weaknesses, he will be unable to offer full support. Some tutors encourage the formation of student groups in which those on the same course can telephone each other to discuss their work, or can meet at regular intervals.

If you need to use specific text books which are recommended by the OU, but not published by it, the nearest university or college library will be of more value than the local library, which is unlikely to have a large range of academic texts. When a large library is inaccessible, books can be ordered from any library using the inter-library loan scheme. You will be asked to complete a form with the details of the required book and a small fee may be charged.

The payment of library fees and the purchase of books raises another problem of studying at the OU — there are no mandatory grants available for its students. The only awards which you can apply for are discretionary awards from the local education authority. In times of economic stringency the authorities tend to reduce the level and number of these awards and, consequently, most OU students have to use their own finances for most of their course. They have to pay their course fees and buy books, there are Summer Schools to pay for, and the transport costs to study centres must be met. Like all university students, it is essential for OU students to get sound financial advice from a bank manager, who will be able to suggest ways of arranging payments. Some banks and building societies offer special loans for OU students.

Most OU students are in full time employment and complete their studies during their free time. If a degree will be an advantage in your job, your employer might agree to meet some of the cost of studying. Combining degree level studies with a full time job is not easy. You will have to decide how many evenings each week will be devoted to your course and you will have to learn to 'switch-off' from any problems at work before launching into a study unit.

A well organised timetable will go some of the way in creating the right framework for study. Follow the principles of timetable making which are outlined in chapter 3. Flexibility is especially vital for students with a family. Most OU students are in their late twenties or thirties and many of them are likely to have young families. The problem of trying to study and bring up children are immense. You might be in the middle of a complex assignment when one child wants attention. A baby might be suddenly ill, or a teenager's record player might be blaring music at all hours. With a rigid timetable you would not be able to cope.

These are the main problems encountered by OU students — the difficulties of combining studies with family life, trying to hold down a job and study, finding enough money to pay for the course, and having access to the right study materials. However, every year thousands of people manage to overcome these problems and succeed in obtaining a degree.

One of the most unusual aspects of the Open University is the lack of the traditional university environment. There are no debates, no discos or late night parties, no political discussions, no union buildings, and no student capers. Because the students are spread throughout the country, and because their ages and backgrounds are so diverse, there is nowhere near the amount of inter-student contact as seen at residential universities.

There is, however, the Open University Students Association. It has a number of local branches which run regular events and meetings for students in particular areas. The main aims of the OUSA are to represent the students to OU authorities and to look after any welfare needs.

The OUSA provides a number of services for students, including insurance and a mail order merchandise department. There is the OUSA hardship fund for students in extreme financial difficulties and a Disadvantaged Student Travel Fund to help pay for transport costs for study tours abroad. OUSA members can also use the National Student Discount Scheme, although the OUSA is not affiliated to the National Union of Students, and they can join a number of clubs and societies.

If you get any problems with your course or your tutor, or discover that you cannot complete your studies because of financial difficulties, then contact the OUSA. Their expert welfare staff will be able to advise you and may even be able to find financial assistance, or persuade the OU authorities to allocate a different tutor.

There is a growing number of postgraduate OU students, although the Open University does not have any formal post-graduate courses. The OU offers the higher degrees of Bachelor, Master, and Doctor of Philosophy as well as a Doctor of Science and Doctor of Letters, all of which are awarded on the basis of research. Students who have gained a minimum of an Upper Second Class Honours degree from any university are entitled to apply for OU postgraduate work. However, students with specialist professional experience may be eligible even if they have lower academic qualifications.

Research degrees of the OU are awarded on acceptance of a

suitable dissertation or thesis, and the principle of obtaining the right number of credits is similar to that for the undergraduate degrees. The advantage of OU research degrees is that they can be taken on a part time basis. This is unusual and is available in only a small minority of residential universities. The majority of OU postgraduates study part time and can therefore work in full time employment while completing research. Occasionally, the research may be part of their job and the employers might pay some of the costs. The university does, however, offer a number of full time research posts if the problems of trying to study on a part time basis seem overwhelming.

Student Directory

At some time during your university career you may need expert personal advice. A talk with your tutor, a student counsellor, or your doctor will always be of value, but there might be occasions when the help of these people is not quite what you want.

There is a large number of organisations to which you can turn. Many of them function on a local basis and their addresses will be in the local telephone directory or Yellow Pages. However, listed here are most of the major organisations which you might need to contact during your days as a student.

Advisory Centre for Education
18 Victoria Park Square
Bethnal Green
London E9

Offers general help and advice about educational matters

Alcoholics Anonymous
11 Redcliffe Gardens
London SW10

Head office of national organisation. Offers help to people who are, or might become, dependent on alcohol

Association of British Adoption and Fostering Agencies
4 Southampton Row
London WC1

Source of information about adoption and fostering

The Association of British Travel Agents (ABTA)
55–57 Newman Street
London W1P 4AH

Represents most travel agents and deals with complaints

Automobile Association
Fanum House
Basingstoke
Hants RG21 2EA

General motoring advice and services to motorists, including roadside repairs

Banking Information Service
10 Lombard Street
London EC3V 5AR

General advice and
information about
banking

British Pregnancy Advisory
Service
Austy Manor
Wootton Warren
Solihull
West Midlands B95 6DA

Local clinics offer
pregnancy tests, abortion
advice and birth control
counselling

Brook Advisory Service
233 Tottenham Court Road
London W1P 9AE

Birth control advice and
help with sexual problems

BUNACAMP
30 Store Street
London WC1E 7BS

Arranges working holidays in
North America for students
and other young people

Campaign for Homosexual
Equality
42a Formosa Street
London W1

Help and advice for
homosexual men and
women

Campaign for Real Ale
(CAMRA)
34 Alma Road
St Albans
Hertfordshire

Information for dedicated
drinkers. Also publishes
an annual Good Beer Guide

Camp America
37 Queens Gate
London SW7 5HR

As for BUNACAMP

Camping Club of Great Britain
and Ireland
11 Lower Grosvenor Place
London SW1W 0EY

Advice and information
on camping holidays

Career Analysts
Career House
90 Gloucester Place
London W1H 4BL

The largest commercial
careers guidance company
in the UK

Central Bureau for Educational
Visits and Exchanges
43 Dorset Street
London W1

Advice and information for
students seeking holiday jobs
abroad. Publish annual guide to
working holidays

Central Council for the Disabled
34 Eccleston Square
London SW1

Will help disabled students
with any problems related to
their handicap

Citizens Advice Bureau
110 Drury Lane
London WC2 5SW

Local office will offer help
and advice on any matter

Citizens Rights Office
1 Macklin Street
London WC2

Help with social security
and income problems

Council for National
Academic Awards (CNAA)
344–354 Grays Inn Road
London WC1X 8BP

Administers the examination
system and awards degrees to
students at polytechnics

Department of Education
and Science
Elizabeth House
39 York Road
London SE1

The government department
responsible for education
policy and development

Endsleigh Insurance Services Ltd
Endsleigh House
Cheltenham Spa
Gloucestershire GL50 3NR

Insurance company designed
to meet needs of students.
The only company to get
the backing of the National
Union of Students

Equal Opportunities
Commission
Overseas House
Quay Street
Manchester M3 3HN

Help for people who think
they are being discriminated
against as a result of their sex

Family Planning Association
27–35 Mortimer Street
London W1N 7RJ

Medical advice on birth
control and any associated
problems

Family Planning Association   As above
of Northern Ireland
47 Botanic Avenue
Belfast
Northern Ireland

Gay Switchboard   A twenty-four hour Samaritan
01-837-7324   style service for people who are,
                                   or think they are, homosexual

Grapevine   Sex education group offering
296 Holloway Road   advice and information
London N7

Independent Assessment and   Vocational guidance and
Research Centre   advice
57 Marylebone High Street
London W1M 3AE

Justice Against the Identification Helps people in trouble with
Laws (JAIL)   the police
271 Upper Street
London N1

Law Society   Will deal with complaints
113 Chancery Lane   against solicitors and
London WC2A 1PL   barristers

Law Society of Scotland   As for Law Society
26 Drumsheugh Gardens
Edinburgh E3

Life   An anti-abortion group which
35 Kenilworth Road   also offers advice to pregnant
Leamington Spa   women undecided about
Warwickshire   abortion

London Student Travel   The largest travel bureau
117 Euston Road   providing cheap travel and
London NW1 2SX   holidays to students

Manpower Services Commission   Advice about employment
Selkirk House   and training schemes
166 High Holborn
London WC1V 6PF

Marriage Guidance Council
Herbert Gray College
Little Church Street
Rugby

Local branches offer advice
to couples with relationship
or sexual problems

National Council for Civil
Liberties
186 King's Cross Road
London WC1X 9DE

Help and information to
protect your freedom

National Council for One
Parent Families
255 Kentish Town Road
London NW5 2LX

Advice for people attempting
to bring up children alone

National Union of Students
3 Endsleigh Street
London WC1H 0DU

The union which represents
all students. Deals with grants
and conditions etc. Provides
help about any student matter

NUS Marketing
University of London Union
Malet Street
London WC1E 7HY

Operates the National Student
Discount Scheme and Great
Stuff Records

Office of Fair Trading
Field House
Breams Buildings
London EC4A 1PR

Explains laws about retailing
and deals with complaints

The Open University
Walton Hall
Milton Keynes MK7 6AA

Offers degree level courses for
all, regardless of qualifications.
Study is by part time
correspondence courses

The Open University
Students Association
Sherwood House
Sherwood Drive
Bletchley
Milton Keynes MK3 6HN

Represents all OU students
and provides a number of
services and clubs

Police Complaints Board
Waterloo Bridge House
Waterloo Road
London SE1 8UT

Deals with all complaints
against the police

Rape Crisis Centre
PO Box 42
London N6 5BU

Moral support and advice for women who have been raped or assaulted. Has a twenty-four hour emergency service on 01-340-6145

Release
1 Elgin Avenue
London W9 3PR

Help for people in trouble with the police. Also advice and information on drugs

Royal Automobile Club
PO Box 100
RAC House
Lansdowne Road
Croydon CR9 2JA

General motoring advice and services to motorists, including roadside repairs

Scottish Council for Civil Liberties
146 Holland Street
Glasgow G2

As National Council for Civil Liberties

Scottish Marriage Guidance Council
58 Palmerston Place
Edinburgh EH12 5AZ

As Marriage Guidance Council

Scottish Youth Hostels Association
7 Glebe Crescent
Stirling

Holiday accommodation for visitors to Scotland

Sexual Problems of the Disabled
Brook House
2–16 Torrington Place
London WC1

Help and advice on sexual matters for disabled men and women

Standing Conference on Drug Abuse
3 Blackburn Road
London NW6

Will advise on sources of help for people with drug problems

Trades Union Congress
Congress House
Great Russell Street
London WC1B 3LS

Represents individual unions and will give advice and information about trade unionism

TSB Information Service Freepost 3 Copthall Avenue London EC2	Information on student banking
Universities Central Council on Admissions (UCCA) PO Box 28 Cheltenham Gloucestershire GL50 1HY	Administers all applications for first degrees
Womens National Cancer Control Campaign 1 South Audley Street London W1	Advice about cancer, but especially breast and cervical cancer
Youth Hostels Association Trevelyan House 8 St Stephens Hill St Albans Hertfordshire	Holiday accommodation especially for young people
Youth Hostels Association of Northern Ireland 93 Dublin Road Belfast	As for Youth Hostels Association

In addition to these sources of advice and information help will be available in your local town. The addresses of the following organisations can be found in your local telephone directory.

Careers Service	Run by county councils and provides the same sort of services as the university careers office
Consumer Advice Centre	Help with consumer problems
Family Practitioner Committee	Deal with complaints against doctors
Inland Revenue Office	Information about tax matters

Libraries	County libraries provide lists of information to meet the needs of different areas
Local Authority	District and borough councils have information offices which deal with local matters
Members of Parliament	Most MPs meet their constituents in regular 'surgeries' to discuss problems and complaints
Police Station	Duty officers will deal with any problem you have
Rent Officer	At town hall to deal with complaints about rented accommodation
Rent Tribunal	Get the address from the Citizens Advice Bureau. The tribunal will deal with complaints from people in rented accommodation where the landlord lives on the premises
The Samaritans	Confidential help for people with personal or emotional problems. Twenty-four hour telephone service
Social Security Office	Help for people in severe financial hardship
Trustee Savings Bank	Help on student banking and your money problems
Unemployment Benefit Office	Arranges cash benefits for the unemployed

The nave of Birmingham Cathedral. Formerly the Church of St Philip, the cathedral was designed by the Baroque architect Thomas Archer in the early eighteenth century

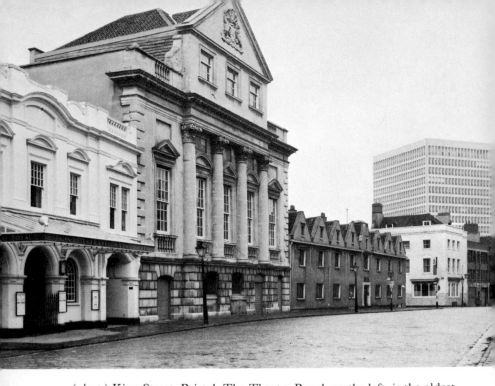

(*above*) King Street, Bristol. The Theatre Royal, on the left, is the oldest theatre in England still holding performances; (*below*) Nevile's Court, Trinity College, Cambridge, showing the magnificent Wren library which was completed in 1684

Further Advice

Because there are so many areas involved it has not been possible to explain in this book every detail of the different aspects of living at college. Fortunately there are a number of specialist books which deal with particular facets of student life in more detail. The list given below is by no means exhaustive, but can be used as a guide to what is available. The books are listed according to the chapters of 'Guide to Student Life Away from Home', and some specialist reference books are also included.

Preparing to go

The Alternative Prospectus of Universities and Polytechnics V. Payne and V. Lipschitz, Wildwood House, London. 1977

Compendium of Advanced Courses in Colleges of Further and Higher Education Regional Advisory Councils, London. Annually

Compendium of University Entrance Requirements The Association of Commonwealth Universities, London. Annually

Degree Courses Guide Careers Research and Advisory Centre, Robsons Press, Cambridge. Annually

Directory of First Degree and Diploma of Higher Education Courses CNAA, London. Annually

First Year at the University B. Truscott, Faber and Faber, London. 1964

The Grants Register Ed. R. Turner, Macmillan, London. Every two years

The Realities of University Life R. Kingsbury, Universities Tutorial Press, London. 1974

Which Degree Haymarket, London. Annually

Coping to begin with

Up to Expectations Nuffield Foundation. 1976

Studying

How to Study H. Maddox, Pan, London. 1975

A Student's Guide to Efficient Study D. E. James, Pergamon, London. 1967

The Student's Guide to Success W. Fisher Cassie and T. Constantine, Macmillan, London. 1977

Study to Succeed P. Hills, Pan, London. 1976

Looking after yourself

Cooking in a Bedsitter K. Whitehorn, Penguin, London. 1977

Taking Off P. Townsend, Pan, London. 1980

Women's Rights: A Practical Guide A. Coote and T. Gill, Penguin, London. 1977

Love and physical relationships

The Fertile Years Wendy Cooper, Arrow Books, London. 1980

The Joy of Sex A. Comfort, Quartet Books, London. 1974

Make it Happy: What Sex is all About J. Cousins, Penguin. 1980

Politics

Student Politics and Higher Education D. Jacks, Lawrence and Wishart, London. 1972

Careers and postgraduate studies

The Annual Guide to Graduate Opportunities (GO) New Opportunity Press

Directory of Opportunities for Graduates (DOG) Business and Career Publications. Annually

Directory of Postgraduate and Post-experience Courses CNAA, London. Annually

Graduate Employment and Training (GET) Hobsons Press. Annually

HMSO Careers Guides Her Majesty's Stationery Office

Schedule of Postgraduate Courses The Association of Commonwealth Universities. Annually

Handbook of Free Careers Information in the United Kingdom Careers Consultants Ltd

In addition to these books there are a number of useful leaflets and booklets, obtainable from the social security office, the unemployment benefit office, and other government agencies.

You will need to keep yourself informed throughout your university career. Read your union handbook, the university or polytechnic prospectus, and the student newspaper.

City Centre Maps

Central Cambridge
Public buildings and places of interest

1 **Christ's College 1505**
2 **Senate House** A fine building of 1722–30 by James Gibb, noted for its wood and plasterwork
3 **Clare College 1326**
4 **Clare Hall**
5 **Corpus Christi College 1352**
6 **Darwin College 1964**
7 **Downing College 1749**
8 **Emmanuel College 1584**
9 **Fitzwilliam College 1869**
10 **Gonville (1348) & Caius College (1557)**
11 **University Arts Facilities**
12 **Jesus College 1496**
13 **Kings College & Chapel 1441**
14 **Lucy Cavendish Collegiate Society**
15 **Magdalene College 1542**
16 **New Hall: Women's College 1954**
17 **Newnham College: Women's College 1871**
18 **Pembroke College 1347**
19 **Peterhouse College 1284**
20 **Queens' College 1448 to 1465**
21 **Ridley Hall Theological**
22 **St Catharine's College 1473**
23 **St Edmund's House**
24 **St John's College 1511**
25 **Selwyn College 1882**
26 **Sidney Sussex College 1596**
27 **Trinity College 1546**
28 **Trinity Hall 1350**
29 **Wesley House Theological**
30 **Westcott House Theological**
31 **Westminster College Theological and Cheshunt College**
32 **University Library** An impressive design of 1931–4 by Sir Gilbert Scott
33 **Great St Mary's Church** The University church (1478–1514) with a fine tower and some Georgian screenwork
34 **Holy Sepulchre, Round Church** Dates from 1104 and is the oldest of the surviving round churches in England. Mainly Norman it has been drastically restored
35 **Little St Mary's Church** Mostly fourteenth-century in decorated style
36 **St Bene't's Church** Retains a notable early eleventh-century Saxon tower, the oldest building in Cambridge
37 **Cambridge & County Folk Museum**
38 **Fitzwilliam Museum**
39 **Museum of Classical Archaeology**
40 **Scott Polar Research Institute**
41 **Sedgwick Museum of Geology**
42 **University Museum of Archaeology and Ethnology**
43 **University New Museums Site,** includes museum of Zoology and **Whipple Science Museum**

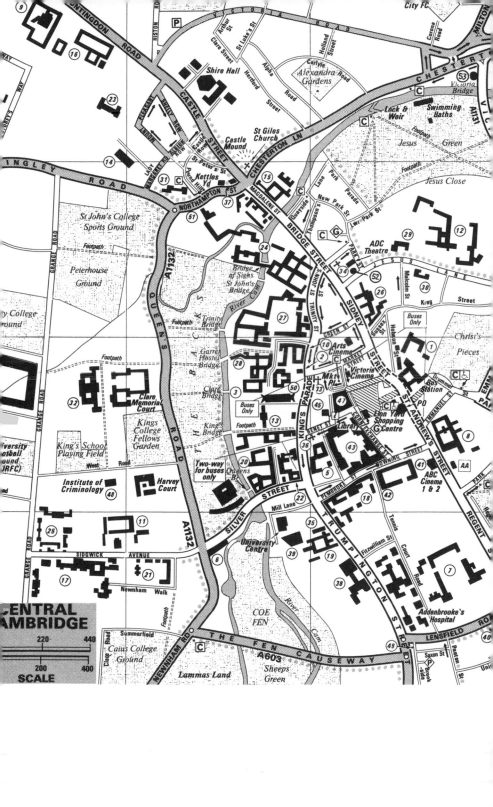

CENTRAL CAMBRIDGE

SCALE

220 — 440

200 — 400

City FC

Corona Road

Milton

Arthur St
St Luke's St
Clare Street

HUNTINGDON ROAD

HISTON ROAD

P

Holland Street

Alpha Road

Hertford Street

Carlyle Alexandra Road Gardens

CHESTERTON

VICTORIA

Victoria Bridge

A1131

Shire Hall

CASTLE STREET

Lock & Weir

Swimming Baths

St Giles Church

Castle Mound

CHESTERTON LN

Jesus Green

St Peter's St

Footpath

Jesus Close

INGLEY ROAD

ROAD

Pound Hill

Kettles Yd

NORTHAMPTON ST

MAGDALENE ST

Footpath

Jesus Lane

BRIDGE STREET

New Park St

Lwr Park St

ADC Theatre

Malcolm St

St John's College Sports Ground

Footpath

GRANGE ROAD

A1132

Peterhouse Ground

St John's Bridge

Bridge of Sighs

River Cam

Trinity Bridge

Footpath

Garret Hostel Bridge

Clare Bridge

Buses Only

Footpath

King's Bridge

Two-way for buses only

Queens Br

Silver Street

Mill Lane

University Centre

SIDNEY STREET

TRINITY STREET

GREEN ST

Sussex St

Hobson St

King Street

Christ's Pieces

Arts Cinema

Mkt Pl.

Victoria Cinema

Market Street

Petty Cury

Lion Yard Shopping Centre

Library

CORN EXCHANGE

KING'S PARADE

BENE'T ST

PEMBROKE STREET

DOWNING STREET

St ANDREW'S STREET

Drummer Station

PO

EMMANUEL ST

AA

ABC Cinema 1 & 2

REGENT

Fitzwilliam St

Tennis Court Road

TRUMPINGTON STREET

THE BACKS

KING'S

School Playing Field

Kings College Fellows Garden

West Road

Institute of Criminology

Harvey Court

SIDGWICK AVENUE

Newnham Walk

Summerfield

GRANGE ROAD

y College round

versity otball tch JRFC)

NEWNHAM RD

A1132

University Centre

COE FEN

River Cam

THE FEN CAUSEWAY

A603

Lammas Land

Sheeps Green

Caius College Ground

Clare Road

Addenbrooke's Hospital

LENSFIELD ROAD

Saxon St

Break-side

9 16 23 14 31 37 51 24 27 28 32 3 50 13 45 47 43 36 10 2 5 6 20 22 35 39 19 38 7 11 25 21 17 48 1 52 26 29 30 12 34 8 41 42 18 40 49 15 53

Central Birmingham
Public buildings and places of interest

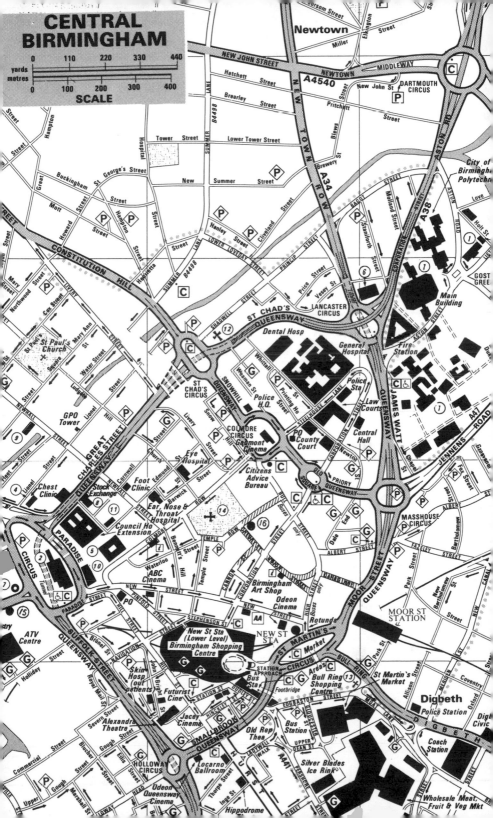

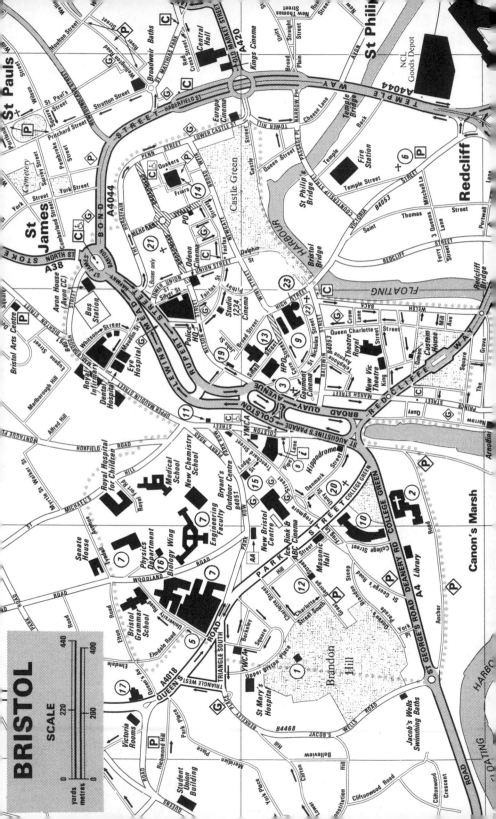

Bristol

Public buildings and places of interest

1 **Cabot Tower** A 150-ft high tower on the summit of Brandon Hill. Built 1897–98 on the four hundredth anniversary of John Cabot's discovery of the mainland of North America at Labrador

2 **Cathedral** Founded as an Augustinian monastery in 1140, it has developed continuously over the past 800 years, with examples of Norman, Early English, Gothic and Victorian architecture

3 **St Stephen's Church**

4 **Chatterton House** The birthplace of Thomas Chatterton (1752–70) the famous boy poet

5 **City Museum and Art Gallery**

6 **Temple Church** A ruined fifteenth-century church with a leaning tower

7 **University**

8 **Colston Hall** One of the finest concert halls in the country

9 **Corn Exchange** In front of the building (1743) are four bronze pillars known as 'Nails' which were at one time used by merchants to complete cash transactions

10 **Council House**

11 **Foster Almshouses** Nineteenth century

12 **The Georgian House,** with eighteenth-century decor

13 **Guildhall** Now used as the Court House

14 **Quakers Friars** Once a Dominican Friary, it has a fourteenth-century roof

15 **Red Lodge** Sixteenth-century house, altered in the early eighteenth century with oak carvings and furnishings of both periods

16 **Royal Fort House** An eighteenth-century merchant's house

17 **Royal West of England Academy**

18 **SS Great Britain** Built by Isambard Kingdom Brunel in 1843, it was the largest iron ship of its time. Salvaged from the Falkland Islands in 1970

19 **St John's Church and Old City Gate** Fourteenth-century church built above the gate which has statues of Brennas and Belinus, mythical figures of the founders of Bristol

20 **St Marks** The Lord Mayor's Chapel, founded in 1220, is noted for its monuments and vestry

21 **Wesley's Chapel** Dating from 1739, it is the oldest Methodist Chapel in the world and was built by John Wesley whose statue is outside

22 **St Nicholas Church and City Museum** Contains the history of Bristol from its beginning until the Reformation

i **Tourist Information Centre**
Trustee Savings Bank

23 35 High Street

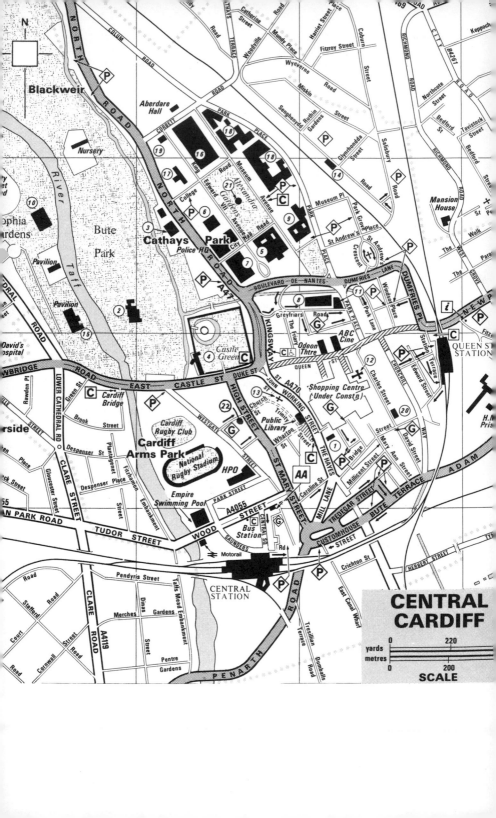

Central Cardiff

Public buildings and places of interest

1 **Arlington Galleries, Oxford Arcade** A permanent exhibition of eighteenth and nineteenth-century paintings
2 **Blackfriars Priory** There are slight remains of this old priory
3 **Cardiff College of Music and Drama**
4 **Castle** An impressive Norman and Victorian structure, retaining a twelfth-century shell keep and thirteenth-century gate-tower. The Victorian buildings contain richly decorated state apartments. The octagon tower is fifteenth-century
5 **City Hall** An imposing building of 1904, with a dome and a 200ft high tower. The marble hall contains statues
6 **County Hall** A fine building of 1910
7 **Law Courts** The building dates from 1894
8 **Municipal Buildings** Information Bureau
9 **National Museum of Wales** A pillared and domed building completed in 1927. It contains highly interesting archaeological and art collections, a gallery of Welsh Folk Life and also botanical and zoological collections
10 **National Sports Centre** An impressive sports complex opened in 1972
11 **New Theatre**
12 **St David's Cathedral (RC)** Contains a notable altar of marble and alabaster
13 **St John's Church** Restored in the nineteenth century, this church has a notable fifteenth-century tower. Much of the building displays thirteenth to fifteenth-century work, and there is Renaissance screenwork in the north chapel
14 **Sherman Theatre**
15 **Sophia Gardens Pavilion and Conference Centre**
16 **Temple of Health and Welsh Office** This building of 1938 contains various organisations responsible for Welsh affairs
17 **Temple of Peace** A building of 1938, with an impressive temple of black and gold marble, housing the National Book of Remembrance
18 **University College**
19 **University of Wales Institute of Science and Technology** The original buildings date from 1916
20 **Welsh Arts Council**
21 **Welsh National War Memorial**
i **Welsh Tourist Board Information Centre**
Trustee Savings Bank
22 119 St Mary Street

Central Belfast

Public buildings and places of interest

1 **Albert Memorial Clock Tower, Victoria Street**

2 **Belfast Bank, Waring Street** The oldest public buildings in Belfast. They occupy the old Exchange and Assembly Rooms where the Harp festival of 1792 took place and were transformed into a handsome building of Renaissance-revival style by Lanyon

3 **Carlisle Memorial Church, Clifton Street**

4 **Christ Church (CI), College Sq North**

5 **City Hall, Donegall Square** White Linen Hall was replaced in function by this large quadrangular building of Portland limestone, whch was designed by Brumwell Thomas in 1906. It is Renaissance in style and is ranged around a central courtyard. Italian marble was used to line the walls of the impressive entrance hall, which is floored with black and white marble and includes a fine staircase lit by stained glass windows. The gardens contain various statues and monuments

6 **Clifton House or Old Charitable Institute, North Queen Street** Said to have been the work of Robert Joy, a Belfast paper merchant, this fine structure is considered a good example of Irish Georgian public building. The main body of the building was built in 1771

7 **Custom House, High Street** This Corinthian-style structure is often considered the city's finest public building and stands near the point where the culverted River Farset flows into the Lagan. It dates from 1857 and was designed by Sir Charles Lanyon in the Italian style after Palladio. Anthony Trollope, the nineteenth-century novelist, worked here as a surveyor's clerk in 1841

8 **Linenhall Library, Donegall Sq North** This library was founded in 1788 as the Belfast Society for Promoting Knowledge. Its superb collection of books relates to Ireland in general, the linen trade in particular and many other subjects of general and historic interest

9 **Municipal College of Technology, College Sq East** This school is housed in a Portland stone building situated in the grounds belonging to the Royal Belfast Academical Institute. The College, built between 1900 and 1910, is equipped to train students in various manufacturing techniques

10 **Old Museum, College Sq North** A four storey stucco building erected in 1831 by Duff and Jackson. There is a substantial collection of stuffed wild birds and Irish antiques

11 **Old Presbyterian Oval Church, Rosemary Street** Built in 1783, when John Wesley preached here in 1789 he said it was the 'completest place of worship I have ever seen'

12 **Royal Belfast Academic Institution, College Sq North** Designed by Sir John Soane, founded in 1807 by the Presbyterians and included a small medical department in its curriculum

13 **Royal Courts of Justice, Oxford Street** This building of Portland stone was opened in May 1933 as a gift from the British parliament. It was designed by J. G. West and includes accommodation for the 'Four Courts' including the Court of Appeal

14 **St Anne's Cathedral (CI), Donegall Street** Completed in 1927, to replace the parish church of St Anne. The interesting nave pavement is a harmonious blend of black marble from Kilkenny and Galway, white marble from Recess, Clifden and Dunlewy, plus the red marble of Cork. The mosaic roof is formed of 150,000 pieces of glass arranged to represent the Creation

15 **St George's Church (CI), High Street**

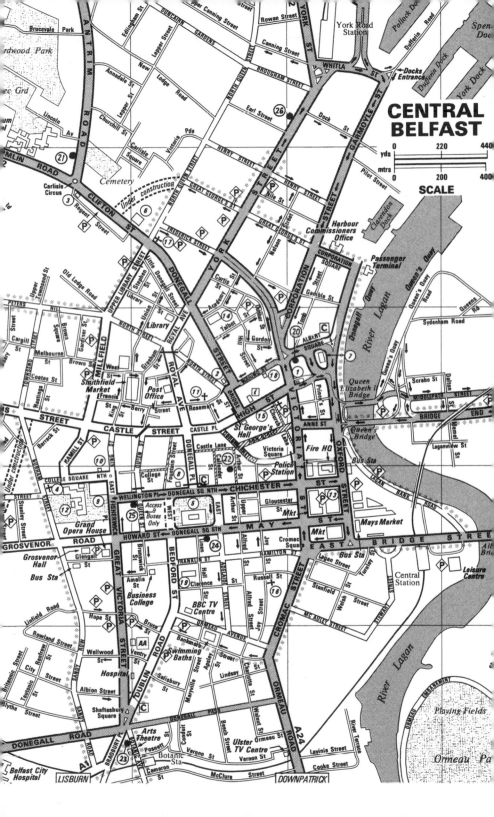

CENTRAL BELFAST

SCALE

yds 0 · 220 · 440

mtrs 0 · 200 · 400

Bruevale Park
rdwood Park
Hardwood Park
ee Grd
um
rd
Lincoln Av
Churchill St
ANTRIM ROAD
Eglinton St
Annadale St
New Lodge Road
Lepper St
Lepper St
Upper Canning Street
DUNCAIRN
GARMOYLE
Canning Street
Rowan Street
Upper Townsend St
Old Lodge Road
PETERS HILL
Brown Square
Gardner St
Cargill St
Melbourne St
Coates St
Hastings St
Brown St
West St
Smithfield Market
Francis St
King St
Berry St
MILLFIELD
NORTH STREET
Library
Gresham St
ROYAL AVE
DONEGALL STREET
UPPER LIBRARY STREET
Little Donegal St
Stephen St
Union St
Rowland Street
Stanley Street
Durham St
Barrack St
Ramill St
CASTLE STREET
Queen St
COLLEGE SQUARE NTH
Linfield Road
Grosvenor Hall
Bus Sta
Glengall St
GROSVENOR ROAD
GREAT VICTORIA STREET
Grand Opera House
Wellington Pl
COLLEGE SQUARE EAST
CHICHESTER
HOWARD ST
DONEGALL SQ NTH
DONEGALL SQ WEST
DONEGALL SQ STH
Amelia St
Business College
Hope St
Bruce
Ormeau
BBC TV Centre
Brunswick St
BEDFORD ST
FRANKLIN ST
Clarence
Hall
Adelaide
GREAT VICTORIA STREET
DUBLIN ROAD
SANDY
Wellwood St
Ventry
AA
Hospital
Albion Street
Salisbury
Apsley
Maryville
SHAFTESBURY
Shaftesbury Square
Botanic St
Arts Theatre
Bradbury
Posnett
Botanic Sta
Vernon St
Cameron
McClure Street
LISBURN
DONEGALL ROAD
A1
Belfast City Hospital
Botinmic St
Teutonic St
Blythe St
Renfrew St
City St
Street
Street
Rowland Street

York Road Station
Pollock Doc
Dufferin Road
Spen Doc
Barnes
SAUNDERS
Rowan Street
NORTH QUEEN STREET
Canning Street
BROUGHAM STREET
WHITLA
Docks Entrance
Dufferin Dock
York Dock
Earl Street
Dock St
Nile St
Henry St
Henry Street
Nelson St
Gamble St
Corporation St
Pilot Street
Harbour Commissioners Office
Clarendon Dock
Passenger Terminal
Queen's Quay
Queen's Road
Queens Rd
Sydenham Road
River Lagan
Albert Square
Queen Elizabeth II Bridge
Queen's Quay
Prince's
ANN ST
Fire HQ
Queen's Bridge
Oxford St
Bus Sta
Scrabo St
Dalton St
BRIDGE END
Lagan St
Lagan view St
Mays Market
LAGAN BANK ROAD
EAST BRIDGE STREET
Central Station
Stanfield St
Bus Sta
Walsh St
Gloucester St
Gloucester St Mkt
Arthur St
Victoria Square
Police Station
May St
Cromac Square
Mkt
Arthur
Upper
Russell St
Alfred
Joy St
Stanfield
Lagan Street
McAULEY STREET
CROMAC STREET
Hamilton St
Charlotte St
Lindsay
Walnut St
Beech St
Ormeau St
Ulster TV Centre
Vernon St
Lavinia Street
Cooke Street
DOWNPATRICK
A24
ORMEAU ROAD
ORMEAU AVENUE
Leisure Centre
River Lagan
Playing Fields
Ormeau Pa
EMBANKMENT
River Terrace

Cemetery
Under construction
Carlisle Circus
Clifton St
Regent Street
Frederick Street
North Queen Street
Great Georges St
Carlisle Square
Victoria Pde
Henry Street
Earl Street
Curtis St
Academy St
Talbot St
Gordon St
HIGH ST
DONEGALL STREET
Royal Ave
Union St
North Street
Library
Rosemary St
St Georges Hall
Castle Lane
Castle Pl
Donegall Pl
DONEGALL PL
Post Office
Francis
King St
Berry St
Callender
Arthur St
Bank St
St George's Hall
CASTLE PL
Smithfield Market

3 · 21 · 26 · 6 · 17 · 14 · 20 · C · 7 · 1 · 18 · 11 · 15 · 22 · 10 · 8 · 12 · 9 · 4 · 25 · 5 · 13 · 24 · 19 · 16 · 23

16 **St Malachy's Church (RC), Alfred Street** Designed by Thomas Jackson and completed in 1848, this unusual church has a strange exterior of numerous turrets and battlements. The interior is undoubtedly the most sumptuous in Belfast

17 **St Patrick's Church (RC), Donegall Street** Contains triptych painted in the pre-Raphaelite manner by Sir John Lavery

18 **Ulster Bank, Waring Street** The headquarters of the Ulster Bank occupies a building designed in an Italian-romantic variation on the classic theme by James Hamilton of Glasgow. It was completed in 1860 and features stonework by Thomas Fitzpatrick

19 **Ulster Hall, Bedford Street** This large building by Barre dates from 1860. Nowadays it caters for boxing and wrestling matches, orchestral concerts and religious and political meetings

   Trustee Savings Bank

20 Head Office: 4 Queen's Square
   Branches:

21 16 Antrim Road

22 25 Arthur Street

23 9 Botanic Avenue

24 8 Donegall Square South

25 34 Wellington Place

26 164 York Street

Reading

Public buildings and places of interest

1 **Abbey Remains (AM)** There are only slight remains of this former twelfth-century foundation, the burial place of Henry I

2*i* **Civic Offices and Tourist Information Centre**

3 **College of Technology**

4 **Shire Hall, County Council Offices, Crown Court**

5 **Grey Friars Church** A flint church of the fourteenth century, with a fine west window

6 **Hexagon** multi-purpose entertainments centre

7 **Museum, Art Gallery and Library** Collections of exhibits from the Roman town of Silchester. Also displays of the development of the Thames Valley

8 **University** A modern university, widely known for its Agricultural Faculty, situated in the 600 acre Whitenights Park. The old buildings in London Road are still in use

9 **Reading School**

10 **St Laurence's Church** Dating from the twelfth century, this church has a 111ft high tower, a sixteenth-century font and interesting monuments

11 **St Mary's Church** Rebuilt in 1551, it contains a carved oak gallery (1631) and a rebuilt organ which was at the Great London Exhibition of 1851

   Trustee Savings Bank

12 235 London Road

13 33 Market Place

Central Edinburgh

Public buildings and places of interest

1 **Acheson House** The headquarters of the Scottish Craft Centre is housed in this seventeenth-century mansion

2 **Assembly Rooms and Music Hall**

3 **Castle and Scottish National War Memorial** The historic castle on its commanding site has many Royal associations. The Norman St Margaret's Chapel is Scotland's oldest ecclesiastical building still in use. The Scottish National War Memorial was opened in 1927

4 **City Chambers** Originally erected in 1753 as the Royal Exchange

5 **Canongate Tolbooth** Once a prison and courthouse and dating back to 1591. It has a curious projecting clock

6 **Edinburgh Festival Office**

7 **Floral Clock** This is the oldest floral clock in the world. It dates from 1903

8 **Freemason's Hall**

9 **George Heriot's School** Dates from 1628 and was founded by George Heriot

10 **Gladstone's Land** Built in 1620 it preserves Edinburgh's last arcaded ground floor

11 **Greyfriars Church and Greyfriars Bobby Statue** The church dates from 1612 and is famous for the signing of the National Covenant in 1638. There is also a memorial to the Covenanters. The statue recalls an Edinburgh dog who watched over his master's grave from 1858 to 1872

12 **White Horse Close** An original coaching terminus in which is situated the 'White Horse Inn'

13 **Huntly House** Dates from 1570. It is now the City Museum of local history

14 **John Knox's House** A fifteenth-century house, preserving wooden galleries. Built by the goldsmith to Mary, Queen of Scots, and probably lived in by John Knox

15 **Lady Stairs House** A restored house, built in 1622. It is now a literary museum

16 **Museum of Childhood** Contains an extremely large collection of items relating to childhood in the past

17 **National Gallery of Scotland** Contains a comprehensive collection of paintings of a number of schools

18 **National Library of Scotland** Contains a large collection of books and manuscripts

19 **National Monument and Nelson Monument** Commenced in 1822, but left unfinished. It commemorates the Scottish dead in the Napoleonic Wars and forms a notable viewpoint. The nearby Nelson Monument is 108ft high

20 **National Portrait Gallery and Museum of Antiquities** The Portrait Gallery was founded in 1882 and contains a collection of portraits of famous Scots. The museum contains a representative collection of history and everyday life of Scotland from the Stone Age to modern times

21 **New University**

22 **Old University** A Robert Adam design of 1789 with nineteenth-century additions

23 **Outlook Tower** This tower contains a fine Camera Obscura, which has been in use since 1892

24 **Parliament House** Built 1633–40 but now masked by later buildings. The Hall has a fine hammer-beam roof

25 **Register House** Built between 1774–89 from designs by Robert Adam. It houses the Archives of Scotland

26 **Royal Scottish Academy** Founded in 1826 to promote fine Arts in Scotland

27 **Royal Scottish Museum** Opened in 1866, it contains the United Kingdom's largest display of the decorative arts, natural history, geology and technology under one roof

28 **St Andrew's House Government Offices** New St Andrew's House, Government Offices are situated in St James Centre

29 **St Giles' Cathedral and Mercat Cross** The cathedral is an imposing and lofty Gothic building. The tower is the oldest part and is surmounted by the famous 'Crown' steeple. The ornate Thistle Chapel dates from 1911. The Mercat Cross, which incorporates the original shaft, was erected in 1885 by Gladstone

30 **Usher Hall**

31 **St Mary's Cathedral (RC)**

32 **Scott Monument** A nineteenth-century memorial to the writer, it was designed by George Kemp

33 *i* **Scottish Tourist Board Offices and Tourist Information Centre**
Trustee Savings Bank

34 208 Bruntsfield Place

35 28 Hanover Street

36 165 Lothian Road

37 20 Marshall Street

38 8 St James Centre

39 10 South Clerk Street

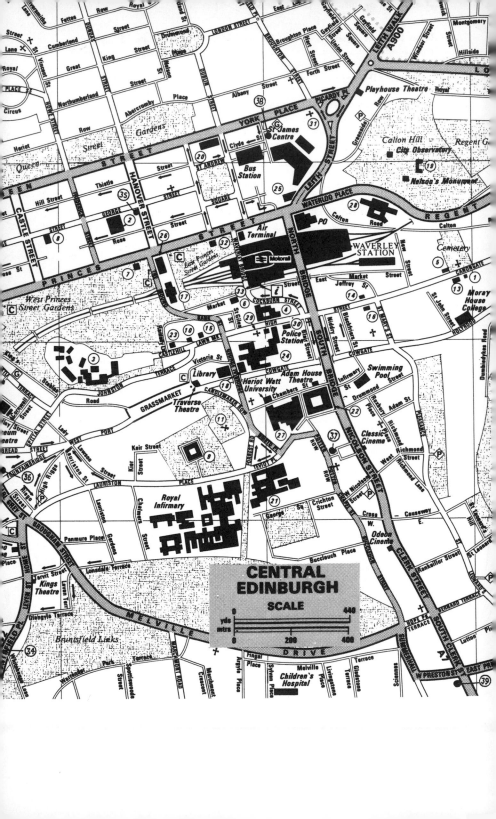

CENTRAL
EDINBURGH

SCALE

yds   440
mtrs

0   200   400

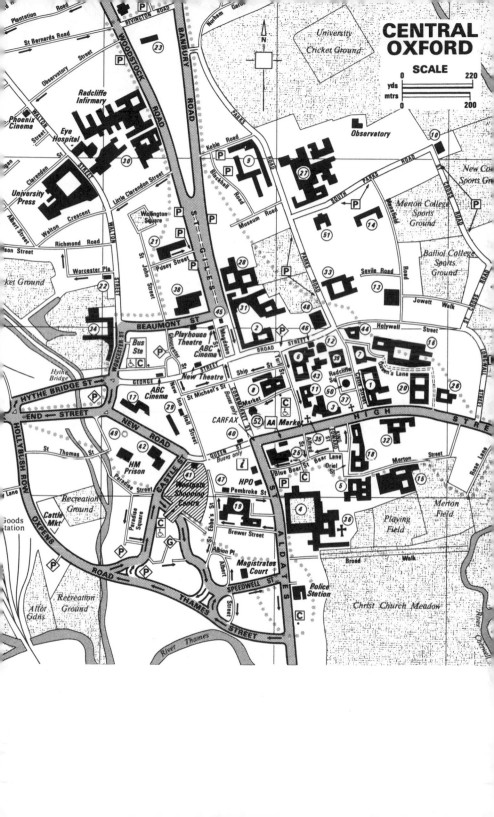

CENTRAL OXFORD

SCALE

yds 0 ——— 220
mtrs 0 ——— 200

Central Oxford
Public buildings and places of interest
1 All Souls College, 1437
2 Balliol College, 1260–6
3 Brasenose College, 1509
4 Christ Church, 1525
5 Corpus Christi College, 1516
6 Exeter College, 1314
7 Hertford College, 1874
8 Jesus College, 1571
9 Keble College, 1870
10 Linacre College, 1962
11 Lincoln College, 1427
12 **Sheldonian Theatre** Designed by Wren and presented to the University in 1669. The Annual Commemoration is held here in late June. Facing it is the early eighteenth-century Clarendon Building by Hawksmoor
13 Manchester College, 1888
14 Mansfield College, 1889
15 Merton College, 1264
16 New College, 1379
17 Nuffield College, 1937
18 Oriel College, 1324–6
19 Pembroke College, 1624
20 Queen's College, 1340
21 Regents Park College, 1957
22 Ruskin College, 1899
23 St Anne's College, 1952
24 St Antony's College, 1948
25 **Town Hall and City of Oxford Museum** The museum reveals the history of Oxford by means of objects, photographs, models and sound
26 St Edmund Hall, c1220
27 **University Museum** Built 1855–60 to house the Natural Science collections. The Pitt–Rivers anthropological collection is notable
28 St John's College, 1555
29 St Peter's College, 1929
30 Somerville, 1879
31 Trinity College, 1554–5
32 University College, 1249
33 Wadham College, 1610–13
34 Worcester College, 1714
35 **All Saints Church** An imposing eighteenth-century structure noted for its panelled ceiling and fine tower
36 **Christ Church Cathedral** A former Augustinian Priory, the structure is mainly eleventh-century but with later additions such as the thirteenth-century cathedral spire. Interior features include Burne–Jones stained glass and a seventeenth-century organ-case and pulpit
37 **St Mary's Church and Oxford Brassrubbing Centre** The University Church of St. Mary the Virgin has a fine spired thirteenth to fourteenth-century tower and a porch of 1637 displaying twisted pillars. This has been the University Church since the fourteenth century. Adjacent is an exhibition of replica brasses, mostly from local churches

38 **Ashmolean Museum** One of the oldest museums in Europe, its treasures include works of art and an extensive collection of coins

39 **Bodleian Library** Second only to the British Museum in the Commonwealth

40 **Carfax Tower** The thirteenth-century tower is all that remains from the former St Martin's Church

41 **City Library and Westgate Shopping Centre**

42 **County Hall**

43 **Divinity School** The Divinity School displays fine Perpendicular work, notably the arched roof with pendant bosses

44 **Indian Institute**

45 **Martyrs' Memorial** Erected by Sir Gilbert Scott in 1841 near the site of the stake where Bishops Cranmer, Ridley and Latimer were burnt

46 **Museum of the History of Science** The finest collection of early astronomical, mathematical and optical instruments in the world, housed in the seventeenth-century Old Ashmolean Museum

47 **Museum of Modern Art**

48 **New Bodleian Library**

49 **Oxford Castle** The tower and mound (not open) are all that remain of the Norman castle built in 1071

50 **Radcliffe Camera** Built by James Gibbs in 1739–49, with a remarkable view from the dome. It is now part of the Bodleian Library

51 **Rhodes House** Founded in 1926 for Rhodes scholars from overseas
Trustee Savings Bank

52 7 Market Street

Central Glasgow
Public buildings and places of interest

1 **Tolbooth Steeple** The surviving portion of the Tolbooth of 1626. It is surmounted by a 'Crown' somewhat similar to examples in Edinburgh and Aberdeen

2 **Cathedral** This twelfth to fifteenth-century structure is considered to be a perfect example of pre-reformation Gothic architecture. The fan vaulting over the tomb of St Mungo in the crypt is notable

3 **City Chambers** This fine building of 1883–8 by William Young in Italian Renaissance style has a rich and lavish interior including a marble staircase and notable banqueting hall

4 **City Hall** A concert hall built in 1841 now refurbished to house the Scottish National Orchestra

5 **George Square** Contains statues of many famous people, including Sir Walter Scott, Queen Victoria, Prince Albert, Robert Burns, James Watt, William E. Gladstone and Sir Robert Peel

6 **Mercat Cross** Erected in 1929, it is a replica of the medieval cross

7 **Merchants Hall Steeple** The only remaining part of the old Merchants House which was built in 1651–9 and is now surrounded by the fish market. The tower is noted for its effect of diminishing storeys

8 **Mitchell Library** Founded in 1874 and contains numerous rare books including a valuable Burns collection

9 **Museum of the Royal Highland Fusiliers** Housed in the regiment's headquarters is a chronological display showing the histories of the Royal Scots Fusiliers and the Highland Light Infantry from their foundation to amalgamation in 1959

10 **Tron Steeple** This forms an arch over the footpath and is all that remains of St Mary's Church, dating from 1637, which was burnt down in 1793 by the Hellfire Club

11 **Provands Lordship** Built in 1471 it is the oldest house in the city. It now houses a museum, mainly of domestic articles and seventeenth and eighteenth-century furniture

12 **St Andrews Cathedral (RC)**

13 **St Vincent Street Church** A striking design of 1857–9 by 'Greek' Thomson

14 **Sheriff Court Buildings** Built in 1842 and enlarged in 1874. They were once the Municipal Buildings

15 **Stirling Library** Contains special collections of books on music and pictorial arts and is housed in the Royal Exchange Building, originally a suburban residence built in 1780

16 **Stow College**

17 **Strathclyde University** One of the leading institutions in the field of applied science

Trustee Savings Bank

18 Head Office: 177 Ingram Street
Branches:

19 39 Bothwell Street

20 101 New City Road

21 93 St Vincent Street

22 411–13 Sauchiehall Street

23 137 West Nile Street

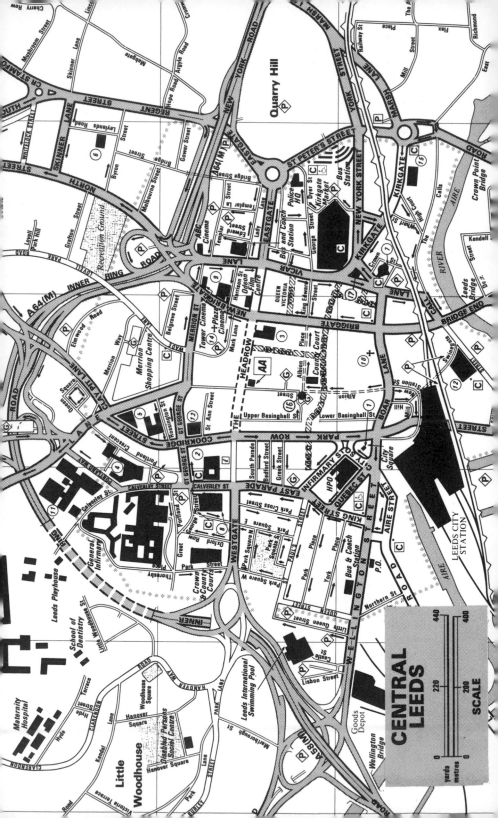

CENTRAL LEEDS

SCALE

Central Leeds

Public buildings and places of interest

1 **Black Prince Statue**
2 *i* **City Art Gallery, Library, Museum and Tourist Information Centre**
3 **City Varieties Theatre** Well known for the BBC series '*The Good Old Days*'
4 **Civic Hall** A modern building, with an imposing porticoed front flanked by twin towers 170ft high
5 **Civic Theatre and College of Art**
6 **College of Building**
7 **Corn Exchange** An unusual oval-shaped building with a domed interior dating from 1861
8 **Town Hall** Designed by Cuthbert Broderick in 1858, it has an impressive colonnaded front and a massive clock-tower rising to 225ft. The triennial Leeds Music Festival is held here
9 **Grand Theatre** A fine, late Victorian building dated from 1878
10 **Holy Trinity Church** This is the only surviving eighteenth-century church in Leeds. Built 1721–7, it is a perfect example of its period
11 **Leeds Polytechnic**
12 **Queen's Hall**
13 **St Anne's Cathedral (RC)** This Gothic-style church was completed in 1904
14 **St John's Church** Dating from 1634, it retains highly interesting Renaissance woodwork, notably the screen and pulpit
15 **St Peter's Parish Church** The oldest church foundation in Leeds, it was rebuilt in 1839–41. It retains a notable pre-Conquest cross
   Trustee Savings Bank
16 PO Box 54, 69 Albion Street
17 110 Kirkgate

Central Exeter
Public buildings and places of interest

1 **Royal Albert Memorial Museum and Art Gallery**
2 **Cathedral of St Peter** A magnificent Norman to Decorated structure; notable features are the twin Norman transeptal towers and the great West Front; minstrels' gallery; carved stone screen; fourteenth-century clock; wood carvings and the wealth of roof bosses
3 **City Walls** Of Roman origin, with alterations 'up to late medieval times. The four gateways survived until the nineteenth century
4 *i* **Civic Centre and Tourist Information Centre**
5 **Custom House** Dating from 1681, it has fine plasterwork ceilings
6 **Guildhall** Britain's oldest municipal building. The present structure, built in 1330, has a roof of 1466 and a magnificent portico completed in 1595
7 **Guildhall Shopping Centre** An impressive shopping precinct opened in 1976, incorporating both the colonnaded frontage and much of the original Civic Hall of 1838, in Queen St, and the thirteenth-century St Pancras Church
8 **Maritime Museum** Over 70 steam and sailing vessels from all over the world, in a setting of quays and old warehouses
9 **Medieval Bridge** The recently excavated and restored remains of the ancient Exe bridge and tower of the former St Edmunds Church can now be visited
10 **Old Mol's House and St Martin's Church** A tall sixteenth-century building, formerly a coffee house. There is a fine oak panelled room. The adjacent fifteenth-century St Martin's Church retains its original oak barrel-vaulted roof
11 **Rougemont Castle and Northernhay Gardens** Situated above the attractive Northernhay Gardens are remains of the Norman Castle (not open) and the County Court. Adjacent to the castle gatehouse are the Georgian Rougemont House (a museum of Exeter and Devon's archaeological history), the beautiful Rougemont Gardens and the City Library
12 **St Catherine's Chapel and Almshouses** The ruined fifteenth-century chapel is now a war memorial
13 **St Mary Arches Church** A mainly twelfth-century church, the only one in Devon to retain a Norman double arcade
14 **St Mary Steps Church** In this church are a Norman font, a good screen and a curious old clock
15 **St Nicholas Priory** A carefully restored eleventh to sixteenth-century Benedictine priory with a Norman undercroft, Tudor room and fifteenth-century kitchen
16 **St Olave's Church** A fourteenth and fifteenth-century church containing an arcade and carvings of the period
17 **St Stephen's Church** Rebuilt in 1664, it has an altar
18 **Tucker's Hall** An old hall, used as a Guild house since 1489 with a fine wagon roof and oak panelling of 1634
19 **Underground Passages** Stone-built vaulted aqueducts dating from the fourteenth century. (Open weekday afternoons, entrance at Paris Street end of Princesshay)
20 **University and Northcott Theatre** A modern university in attractive grounds overlooking the city
21 **Wynard's Almhouses** Attractive almshouses and chapel of 1430 grouped around a central courtyard. (Now council offices)
    Trustee Savings Bank
22 8 Bedford Street
23 175 Cowick Street
24 120 Sidwell Street

Central Liverpool
Public buildings and places of interest

1 **Town Hall** Built 1749–54 to the designs of John Wood the Elder, with enlargements of 1789–92 by James Wyatt

2 **Bluecoat Chambers** Well-restored Queen Anne style building of 1716 and now the headquarters of the Merseyside Arts Association

3 **College of Technology**

4 **Council Offices and Information Bureau**

5 **University**

6 **Dock Board Offices**

7 **Metropolitan Cathedral (RC)** This very impressive modern cathedral of conical shape was designed by Sir Frederick Gibberd and consecrated in 1967. It possesses a central pinnacled lantern tower with stained glass by John Piper and Patrick Reyntians

8 **Philharmonic Hall**

9 **Walker Art Gallery, Museum and City Libraries** The gallery possesses one of the most famous collections of paintings in England while amongst the museum's exhibits are collections on shipping, transport, natural history and also a planetarium. The public libraries are considered one of the oldest and largest in England

10 **St George's Hall** A notable building of 1838–54, possibly the finest Greco–Roman style building in Europe, designed by H. L. Elmes

11 **St John's Beacon** A 450ft high tower, Liverpool's highest building, with a restaurant and observation platform

i **Tourist Information Centre** St John's Precinct
Trustee Savings Bank

12 93 Bold Street

13 19 Brunswick Street

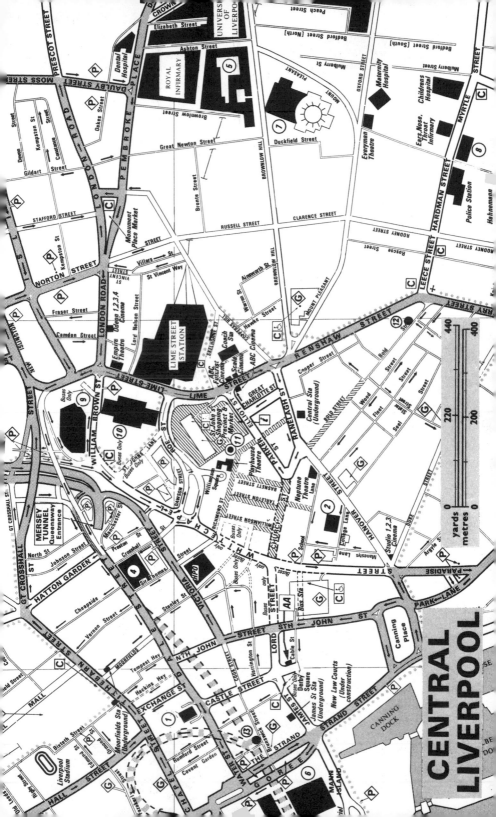

CENTRAL LIVERPOOL

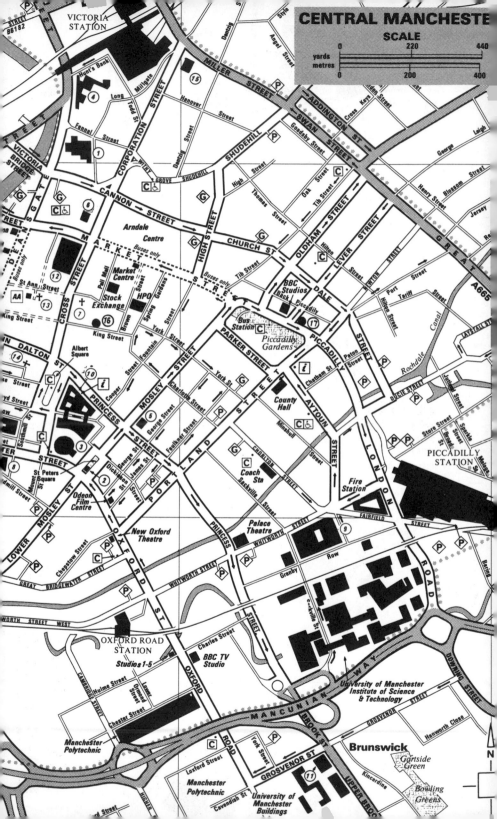

Central Manchester

Public buildings and places of interest

1 **Cathedral** Formerly the Parish Church, this mainly fifteenth-century structure is noted for its fine tower and outstanding carved woodwork

2 **Cenotaph and Garden of Remembrance**

3 **Central Library** This was designed in 1934 in the form of a rotunda and is England's largest municipal library. In the basement is the Library Theatre

4 **Chetham's Hospital, School and Library** A notable fifteenth-century building with modern additions, now an independent grammar school. The free library founded in 1653 claims to be the oldest in England

5 **City Art Gallery and Athenaeum** The art gallery, housed in a building of 1824 designed by Sir Charles Barry, contains Manchester's principal collection of paintings, and smaller collections of pottery and silver. The Athenaeum contains a museum of ceramics, pottery and porcelain

6 **'Wellington' Inn** A picturesque half-timbered structure of the sixteenth-century

7 **Cross Street Chapel** Originally built in 1697 this is the oldest Nonconformist place of worship in Manchester

8 **Free Trade Hall** A fine building rebuilt in 1951 after severe bomb damage. This is the home of the Halle Orchestra

9 **University of Manchester Institute of Science and Technology (Main building)**

10 **Town Hall** A large Gothic building designed by Alfred Waterhouse and opened in 1877. The central tower rises to 280ft and contains a carillon of 23 bells

11 **North Western Museum of Science and Industry** Exhibits include steam and internal combustion engines, machine tools, electrical exhibits, paper making, printing, and textile machinery

12 **Royal Exchange Theatre** An impressive modern theatre housed within the main hall of the former Royal Exchange dating from 1809

13 **St Ann's Church** An early eighteenth-century church in which de Quincey, the writer, was baptised

14 **St Mary's Church (RC)** Known as the 'Hidden Gem' because of its fine altar and hidden location

15 **The New Century Hall**

Tourist Information Centres

i **County Hall extension**

i **Town Hall**

Trustee Savings Bank

16 82 King Street

17 43 Piccadilly

Central Newcastle

Public buildings and places of interest

1 **All Saints' Church** A fine late eighteenth-century church containing the largest memorial brass in England
2 **Black Gate** The thirteenth-century castle gatehouse contains the Bagpipe Museum
3 *i* **Central Library, Northern Arts Gallery and Tourist Information Centre**
4 **City Walls** The longest remaining portion of the thirteenth-century walls, with two towers
5 **Civic Centre** An impressive modern building
6 **Eldon Square Sports Centre and Shopping Precinct** A recently completed development which includes an eight-rink bowling green
7 **Guildhall and Merchants' Court** The Guildhall, dating from 1658, was recased in 1796. The adjoining Merchants' Court contains a seventeenth-century chimney piece
8 **Hancock Museum** One of the finest natural history museums in England
9 **John George Joicey Museum, Holy Jesus Hospital** An almshouse founded in 1681 with displays of arms and armour, period rooms and local history
10 **Laing Art Gallery and Museum** British oil paintings from the seventeenth century onwards, and displays of armour, costumes and local history
11 **University** In the Quadrangle are the Museum of Antiquities which contains Roman remains, the Hatton Gallery with fourteenth- to eighteenth-century European paintings, the Greek Museum housing pottery, bronzes and weapons, and the Mining Museum
12 **Plummer Tower** The restored tower, a part of the medieval city walls, is now a museum
13 **Royal Grammar School**
14 **St Andrew's Church** The city's oldest church, dating from the thirteenth and fourteenth centuries. It contains a fifteenth-century font
15 **St John's Church** A mainly fifteenth-century church with medieval glass and a fine seventeenth-century pulpit
16 **St Mary's RC Cathedral** Designed by Pugin in 1844
17 **St Nicholas' Cathedral** Formerly a parish church. This fourteenth- and fifteenth-century building received cathedral status in 1882. The west tower is surmounted by a notable 'crown' spire, 194ft high
18 **The Keep (Castle)** The massive rectangular 82ft high keep of the city's castle dates from the late twelfth century. There is a small museum
19 **Trinity House** The eighteenth-century courtyard preserves its unusual Dutch character. The interior retains an early eighteenth-century hall and chapel
  Trustee Savings Bank
20 25 Grainger Street
21 12 St Mary's Place
22 264 High Street, Gateshead

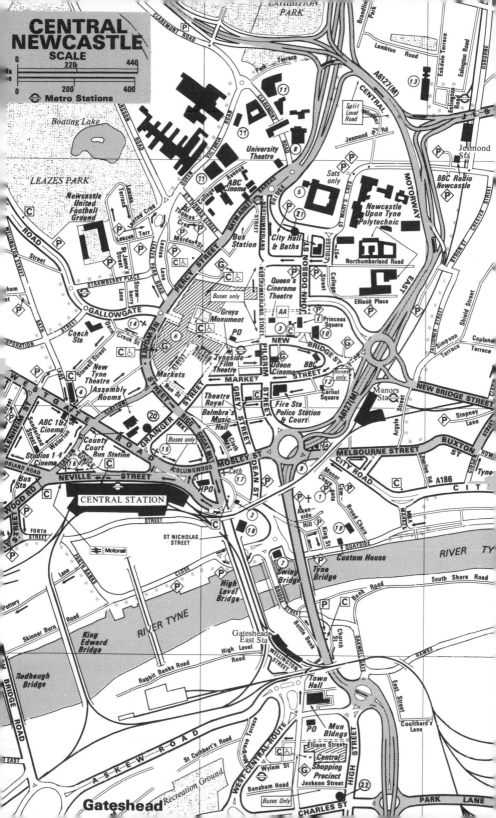

Central Sheffield

Public buildings and places of interest

1 **Cathedral** The cathedral church of Saint Peter and Saint Paul was formerly the parish church which was raised to cathedral status in 1914 and dates from the fourteenth and fifteenth centuries. The sixteenth-century Shrewsbury Chapel contains fine monuments. A new chapel was consecrated in 1948

2 **City Hall** Dating from 1932 it has six halls for meetings and concerts. Of note are the Oval Hall, seating over 2,700 people and the Memorial Hall, a memorial to the fallen of the First World War

3 **Crucible Theatre** A modern theatre, opened in 1971, with seating for 1,000 in the main auditorium

4 **Cutlers' Hall** A Grecian style building dating from 1832. It contains the Cutlers' Company Collection of silver, with examples of craftsmanship dating back every year to 1773. The historic Cutlers' Feast, dating from the early seventeenth century, is held here annually

5 **Former Girls' Charity School** An attractive pedimented house of 1786

6 **Georgian houses in Paradise Square**

7 i **Graves Art Gallery, Central Library and Tourist Information Centre** The Central Library, dating from 1934, is one of the finest in the country and is officially approved as a repository for manorial records and other historical documents. The Graves Art Gallery, in the same building, has examples of Italian, English, and French painting, and the Grice Collection of Chinese Ivories

8 **Sheffield Polytechnic**

9 **Town Hall** Dating from 1897, it has a tower 193ft high, and an impressive grand staircase

10 **University** Dating from 1905 the university has nine faculties. Recent development includes a 19-storey Arts tower

Trustee Savings Bank

11 103 Norfolk Street

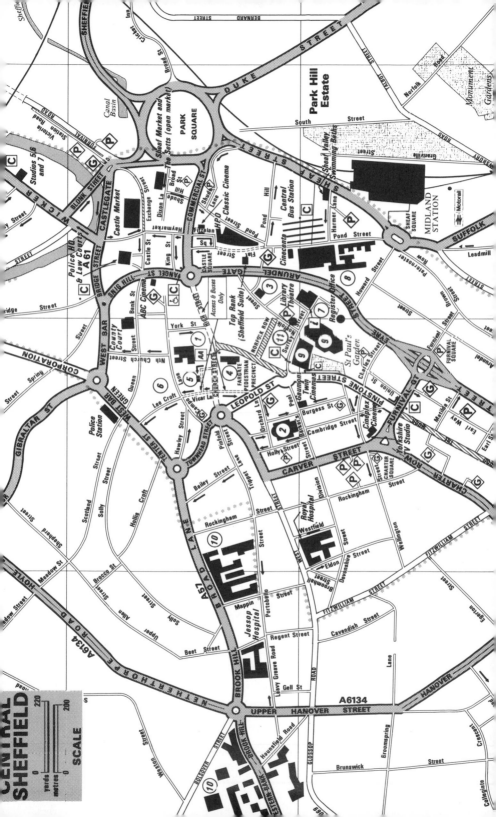

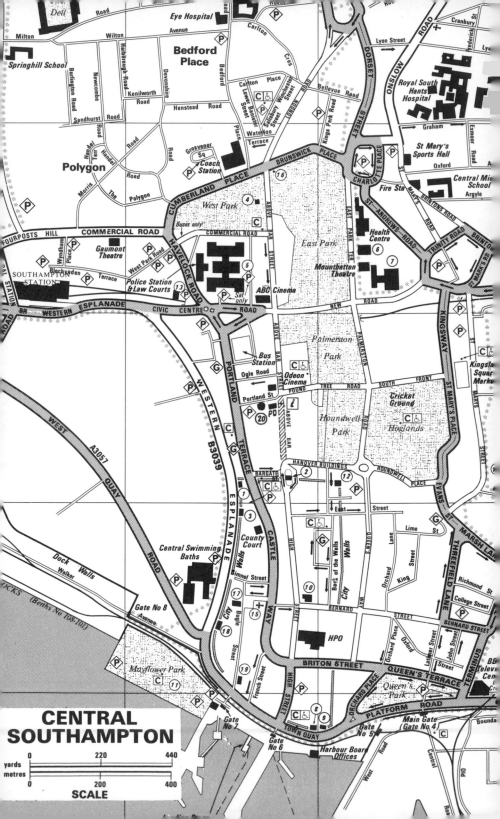

CENTRAL SOUTHAMPTON

SCALE

yards 0 — 220 — 440
metres 0 — 200 — 400

Central Southampton

Public buildings and places of interest

1 **Arundel or Wind Whistle Tower (AM)** One of the towers of the City Wall, which dates from the Norman period

2 **Bargate (AM)** The medieval north gate of the city. Its upper floor, once a guildhall, contains a museum of local interest

3 **Catchcold Tower (AM)** Part of the city walls

4 **Cenotaph**

5 **Civic Centre, Guildhall, Library and Art Gallery** A modern group of buildings, dating from 1932, with a very prominent clocktower

6 **College of Art**

7 **College of Technology** Contains the Mountbatten Theatre

8 **God's House and God's Gate** God's House, or Hospital, was founded in 1185, and contains the restored chapel of St Julian. God's Gate adjoins the God's House Tower

9 **God's House Tower** Dates from the early fifteenth century, and contains the restored chapel

10 **Holy Rood Church** The remains of this church are preserved as a Merchant Navy memorial. The fourteenth-century tower has survived

11 **Mayflower Park** with memorials. The Pilgrim Fathers' Memorial recalls the sailing of the *Mayflower* from the West Quay on 15 August 1620

12 **Polymond Tower** Part of the city walls

13 **R. J. Mitchell Museum** A new museum dedicated to the designer of the famous World War II 'Spitfire'. One of these aircraft is on show in the building

14 **St Mary's Church** Rebuilt and re-dedicated in 1956, it was the origin of the song 'The Bells of St Mary's'

15 **St Michael's Church** The oldest church in the city with parts dating back to 1070. It preserves a rare twelfth-century black marble Tournai font

16 **Titanic Memorial** A memorial to the engineers of the famous liner which struck an iceberg in 1912

i **Tourist Information Centres**

17 **Tudor House Museum** A half-timbered, sixteenth-century mansion containing a museum of antiquarian and historical interest. There is access through the garden to a Norman merchant's house, dating from c1175

18 **West Gate** Dating from the thirteenth century, it led to the Old West Quay, from where the *Mayflower* sailed

19 **Wool House, Maritime Museum** A fine example of a fourteenth-century warehouse, it contains the impressive maritime museum

Trustee Savings Bank

20 30 Portland Street

Central Hull

Public buildings and places of interest

1i **Central Library, Information Bureau, Film Theatre and Tourist Information Centre**
2 **City Hall**
3 **College of Further Education**
4 **Customs and Excise Buildings**
5 **Ferens Art Gallery**
6 **Guildhall and Law Courts**
7 **Holy Trinity Church** A fourteenth- and fifteenth-century structure and one of the largest Parish churches in England. It is noted for its early brickwork, a fine font and a massive tower
8 **Maister's House (NT)** A Georgian merchant's house of 1743 with an impressive staircase and finely carved doors
9 **Municipal Offices**
10 **Regional College of Art**
11 **St Mary's Church** Early fourteenth century, with a brick tower of 1697 later encased in stone
12 **Telephone House**
13 **Town Docks Museum**
14 **Transport and Archaeological Museums**
15 **Trinity House** Formerly the offices of a Guild of Humber Pilotmen. It is now concerned with seamen's welfare. The building dates from 1753 and contains paintings associated with its history
16 **Wilberforce House** An early seventeenth-century mansion where William Wilberforce was born in 1759. Now the Wilberforce Historical Museum
17 **Wilberforce Monument**
  Trustee Savings Bank
18 1–7 George Street

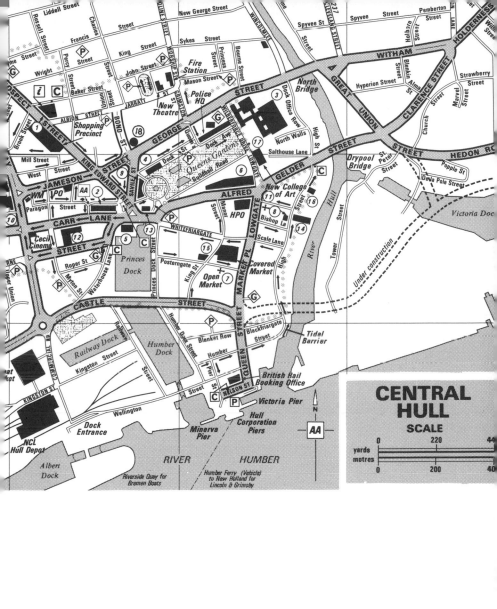

CENTRAL HULL

SCALE

yards
metres

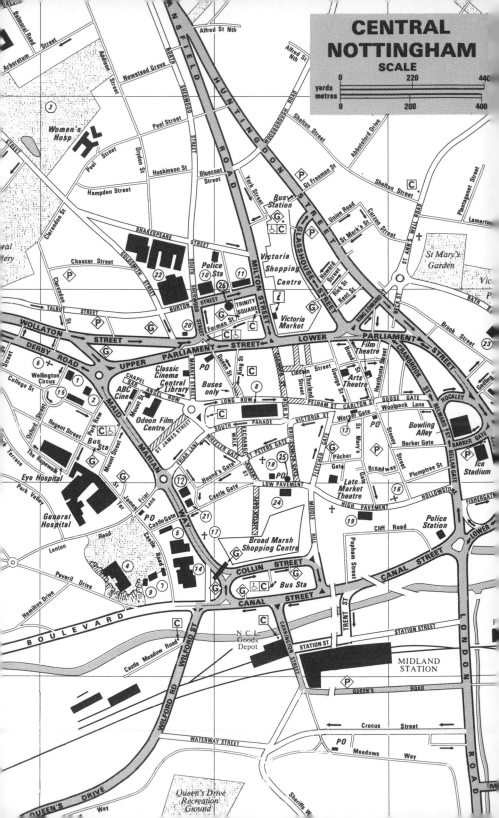

Central Nottingham

Public buildings and places of interest

1 **Albert Hall**

2 **Albert Hall Institute**

3 **Arboretum Park and Aviaries** Renowned for its dahlia border and other flowers in season

4 **Castle** The present castle consists of a seventeenth-century Italianate style mansion, which forms a fine viewpoint, and houses a museum and art gallery. Displays include ceramics, silver, textiles, ethnography, archaeology, seventeenth-to twentieth-century English and Dutch paintings, medieval alabasters, and modern painting and sculpture. Also Regimental Museum of the Sherwood Foresters. Of the medieval castle only the late thirteenth-century gatehouse remains, which has been restored. Near the gateway is a group of statues representing Robin Hood and his Merry Men

5 **Castlegate Museum** An elegant row of Georgian terraced houses displaying costume from seventeenth-century to the present day, textiles, in particular lace for which Nottingham is famed, and dolls

6 **Cathedral (RC)** This is an early work by Pugin, dating from 1842–4

7 **Ye Olde Trip to Jerusalem Inn** This inn bears the date 1189 and is claimed to be the oldest inn in the country

8 **Council House** A fine building of 1927–8, in Portland stone with facade displaying Greek and Roman influence and domed clock tower housing a loud bell known locally as 'Little John'

9 **Brewhouse Yard Museum**

10 **Guildhall**

11 **Mechanics' Institute**

12 **Ye Olde Salutation Inn** A well-preserved and picturesque building of the thirteenth century

13 **Midland Group Arts Centre** Exhibitions of contemporary painting, sculpture, pottery and mixed media

14 **People's College**

15 **Playhouse Theatre** A large modern theatre opened in 1963

16 **St Mary's Church** A large fifteenth-century structure, with a massive tower, Royal Arms of 1710, and some monuments

17 **St Nicholas Church** A church of 1678, with additions of the eighteenth century

18 **St Peter's Church** A mainly fifteenth-century structure, retaining thirteenth-century work in the nave, and with rebuilt chancel of 1870. It features an organ of 1812

19 **Shire Hall** The central block was built to a design by James Gordon of 1770

20 **Theatre Royal** A touring theatre, renovated in 1978

21 **The Royal Children Inn** The sign is made from the shoulder bone of a whale

i **Tourist Information Centre**

22 **Trent Polytechnic (Newton Buildings)**

23 **Victoria Leisure Centre**

24 **Willoughby House** A house built c1730

Trustee Savings Bank

25 Low Pavement

26 9 Trinity Row, Trinity Square

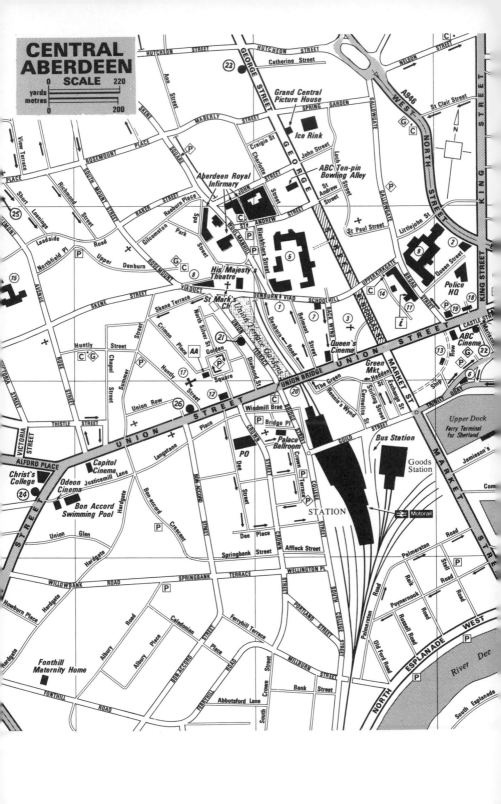

Central Aberdeen
Public buildings and places of interest
1   **Art Gallery, War Memorial and Cowdray Hall**
2   **Civic Arts Centre**
3   **East and West Churches of St Nicholas** Features include Jamesone tapestries
     and the fifteenth-century St Mary's Chapel
4   **Fish Market**
5   **Gordon's College** Founded in 1739 by Robert Gordon
6   **Harbour Offices**
7   **James Dun's House** An eighteenth-century house used as a museum for children
     with a changing programme of exhibitions
8   **Library**
9   **Marischal College (Aberdeen University)** Founded in 1593 the building has an
     impressive frontage of white granite, and houses the University's Anthropological
     Museum
10 **Mercat Cross** Dating from 1668, with relief portraits of Scottish Kings
11 **Municipal Buildings** City of Aberdeen District Council
12 **Music Hall** Two adjoining halls dating from 1820
13 **Provost Ross's House (NTS)** Aberdeen's third oldest house, built in 1593.
     Temporarily closed for conversion to a maritime museum
14 **Provost Skene's House** A seventeenth-century house restored as a museum of
     local history and social life
15 **Rubislaw Academy (Grammar School) and Byron Statue**
16 **St Andrew's Episcopal Cathedral** Mother church of the Episcopal Communion
     in America
17 **St Mary of the Assumption Cathedral (RC)**
18 **Tolbooth** The tower and spire remain of the fourteenth-century Tolbooth. Public
     executions were held here until 1857
i   **Tourist Information Centre** St Nicholas House
19 **Town House** A medieval Gothic building of 1868–74
20 **Union Bridge** One of the widest single span granite arches in Britain
     TSB Aberdeen Savings Bank
21 Head Office: 19 Union Terrace
     Branches:
22 40 Castle Street
23 393 George Street
24 8 Holburn Street
25 138 Rosemount Place
26 226 Union Street
27 70 Victoria Road

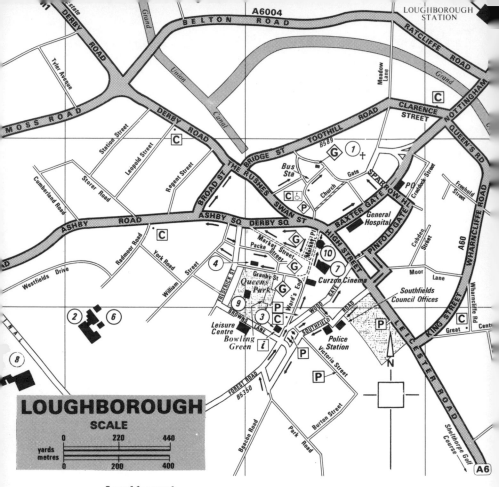

Loughborough

Public buildings and places of interest

1 **All Saints' Parish Church** A fourteenth- and fifteenth-century church noted for its fine tower, includes the Rectory ruins

2 **College of Arts**

3 *i* **John Storer House Community and Tourist Information Centre**

4 **Library**

5 **Loughborough Central Station** Headquarters of the Main Line Steam Trust who have re-opened part of the former GC main line to Leicester. Locomotives and rolling-stock on display

6 **Technical College**

7 **Town Hall**

8 **University (College of Education)**

9 **War Memorial Tower** This has a well-known carillon of 47 bells. It is situated in Queen's Park. The tower is open to the public between 14.00 and 16.00 hours
   Trustee Savings Bank

10 11 Baxter Gate

Index